SIX-SESSION BIBLE STUDY GUIDE + STREAMING VIDEO

THE GREAT MORNING REVOLUTION BIBLE STUDY

Discover a Rhythm of Prayer to Begin Each Day

TARA BETH LEACH

HarperChristian Resources

Published by HarperChristian Resources, 3950 Sparks Drive SE, Suite 101, Grand Rapids, MI 49546, USA. HarperChristian Resources is a registered trademark of HarperCollins Christian Publishing, Inc.

Requests for information should be addressed to customercare@harpercollins.com.

ISBN 978-0-310-17183-6 (softcover)

ISBN 978-0-310-17184-3 (ebook)

HarperChristian Resources titles may be purchased in bulk for church, business, fundraising, or ministry use. For information, please email ResourceSpecialist@ChurchSource.com.

The author is represented by Tom Dean, Literary Agent with A Drop of Ink LLC, www.adropofink.pub.

HarperCollins Publishers, Macken House, 39/40 Mayor Street Upper, Dublin 1, D01 C9W8, Ireland (https://www.harpercollins.com).

Art direction: Ron Huizinga

Cover Design: Emily Weigel

Interior Design: Robin Crosslin

First Printing July 2025 / Printed in the United States of America

25 26 27 28 29 30 /VPI/ 10 9 8 7 6 5 4 3 2 1

A PERSONAL INVITATION

Welcome to *The GREAT Morning Revolution Bible Study*! I'm so excited to journey with you through these six weeks as we explore how to transform our mornings and, ultimately, our lives through intentional time with God at the start of each day.

As someone who once thought being a "morning person" was impossible, I understand the hesitation you might feel. Trust me when I say: If I could train my body to run a marathon and to wake up early with purpose, you can too! This revolution isn't about perfection—it's about presence. It's about creating space at the dawn of each day to meet with God before meeting the demands of your schedule.

I remember vividly those first mornings when my alarm would go off, and every part of me wanted to hit snooze and roll over. The stillness of those early hours felt foreign, even uncomfortable at first. But I promise you, there is a sacred invitation waiting in the morning quiet—a chance to commune with God before the noise of the day drowns out His gentle voice.

In the stillness of the early morning, when the world is still quiet, there is a sacred moment that beckons your soul to awaken. The day is yet untouched by the noise of chaos and clamor, and the heart can commune with God in ways that the rest of the day cannot offer.

This isn't about becoming a superhuman who bounds out of bed at 4 a.m. with a smile (though that might happen!). This is about finding the joy that comes in the morning through God's presence. It's about training ourselves, little by little, to meet God in those first waking moments.

I'm so grateful you've decided to join me on this journey. Let's discover together how beginning with God can transform not just our mornings but our entire lives.

With hope for your mornings,

Tara Beth Leach

CONTENTS

HOW THIS STUDY WORKS

What makes this study unique is that we'll build your morning routine gradually, week by week. I know from experience that trying to change everything at once rarely leads to lasting transformation. Instead, we'll take small, intentional steps that build on each other. We will record our thoughts and experiences and have opportunities to see the documentation of the important and valuable changes in not only our prayer lives but in the relationship God calls us into as we go.

BUILDING YOUR MORNING REVOLUTION

In **Week 1**, you'll establish the foundation—finding your optimal wake-up time (maybe just fifteen minutes earlier than usual), creating a sacred space, and beginning with simple morning stillness.

For **Week 2**, you will add **gratitude** to your routine. You'll continue the practices from Week 1 while learning to begin each day by thanking God for His gifts—both obvious and subtle.

During **Week 3, reflection** will join your growing practice. You'll maintain stillness and gratitude while adding time for honest self-examination and remembrance of God's faithfulness.

In **Week 4**, you'll incorporate **exaltation**—lifting God's name high through various expressions of worship to start your day.

For **Week 5**, you'll learn to bring your requests to God with both boldness and surrender, adding the practice of **asking** to your morning routine.

Finally, in **Week 6**, you'll complete the GREAT Morning framework by embracing **trust**—surrendering control and outcomes to God before facing the day ahead.

By the end of our six weeks together, you'll have established a complete morning practice that includes Gratitude, Reflection, Exaltation, Asking, and Trusting. These elements together form a revolutionary approach to beginning each day in God's presence.

WHAT YOU'LL NEED

For this journey, I recommend:

- ☐ A Bible
- ☐ A journal or notebook
- ☐ This study guide
- ☐ A device to stream my video teaching segments (TV, laptop, phone), or a DVD player (DVD is sold separately if that is your preference.)
- ☐ A quiet, comfortable space where you can meet with God
- ☐ A willingness to try something new, even if it feels challenging at first

INTRODUCTION

JOY COMES IN THE MORNING

(90 MINUTES)

WELCOME AND INTRODUCTION

(10 MINUTES)

For groups meeting for the first time, allow participants to introduce themselves.

Icebreaker: Describe a time when morning brought you clarity or relief after a difficult night. What made that morning significant?

OPENING THEOLOGICAL REFLECTION

(5 MINUTES)

Select a volunteer to read aloud.

Throughout Scripture, morning serves as a powerful theological symbol. From the very beginning in Genesis 1, God establishes a rhythm of evening and morning, with each new day emerging from darkness into light. This pattern reflects God's ongoing work of bringing order from chaos, hope from despair, and life from death.

The prophets and psalmists repeatedly point to morning as the time when God's mercies are experienced anew. Lamentations declares that God's compassions "are new every morning" (3:23), while Psalms speaks of "joy com[ing] with the morning" after a night of weeping (30:5 ESV). These aren't merely poetic sentiments but theological declarations about God's character and His commitment to renewal.

Jesus Himself embraced morning as sacred time, rising "very early . . . while it was still dark" (Mark 1:35) to commune with the Father. In His resurrection, Christ conquered death "early on the first day of the week," making morning forever symbolic of God's victory over darkness (John 20:1).

As we begin this journey into morning prayer, we're not simply adopting a helpful habit. We're participating in a divine pattern woven throughout redemptive history—embracing the theological significance of beginning with God before all else.

OPENING PRAYER

Pray together in unison or select a volunteer:

Faithful God, as we begin this journey of exploring morning prayer, we recognize that we are entering into an ancient pattern established by You. Morning has always been Your time of renewal, revelation, and resurrection. Open our hearts to the theological significance of beginning our days with You. May we experience the joy that comes in the morning as we seek Your face first each day. In Jesus' name, amen.

SCRIPTURE READING BEFORE TEACHING

Read Lamentations 3:19–26 aloud, allowing the full context of the "mercies new every morning" passage to be heard.

VIDEO TEACHING

(20 MINUTES)

Watch Week 1 video "Joy Comes in the Morning" streaming or on DVD.

NOTES

Use the space below to take notes if you'd like.

GROUP DISCUSSION

(45 MINUTES)

Leader, present each prompt, associated passages, and questions in order to the group. Where scripture is to be read, select a volunteer to read aloud to the group.

1. Exploring Biblical Patterns of Morning Prayer

Look at the passages below:

In the morning, Lord, you hear my voice; in the morning I lay my requests before you and wait expectantly (Psalm 5:3).

Very early in the morning, while it was still dark, Jesus got up, left the house and went off to a solitary place, where he prayed (Mark 1:35).

But I cry to you for help, Lord; in the morning my prayer comes before you (Psalm 88:13).

What patterns do you observe about morning prayer in Scripture?

What significance might there be to beginning the day with God?

2. The Theology of Renewal

Read Lamentations 3:19–26 again. This passage was written during Israel's darkest hour—after the destruction of Jerusalem. How does this historical context deepen our understanding of God's mercies "new every morning"?

What does this reveal about God's character in the midst of suffering?

3. Morning as a Spiritual Symbol

Throughout Scripture, morning often symbolizes new beginnings, hope, and God's faithfulness. Look up the following passages, read them independently, examine them, and discuss their theological implications.

- Exodus 16:13–21 (manna in the morning)

- Psalm 30:5 (joy comes in the morning)

- Isaiah 33:2 (God as our strength every morning)

- Mark 16:1–6 (resurrection very early in the morning)

How do these passages shape our understanding of beginning each day with God?

4. The Example of Jesus

In Mark 1:35, we see Jesus rising "very early in the morning, while it was still dark" to pray. This happens after a demanding evening of ministry (Mark 1:21–34) and before another full day ahead (Mark 1:36–39). What does this reveal about Jesus' priorities and the importance He placed on morning communion with the Father?

5. Obstacles to Morning Prayer

What barriers keep you from establishing a consistent morning routine with God?

How might these barriers reflect deeper spiritual struggles?

What scriptural principles might help overcome these obstacles?

6. **Theological Reflection for Modern Application**

   How does a theological understanding of morning as God's time of renewal challenge our cultural perspectives on mornings as merely a time to "get going" or "be productive"?

   How might this shift in perspective transform your approach to each new day?

7. **First Steps of Transformation**

   Based on today's discussion, what is one specific change you feel called to make in your morning routine?

   What scriptural truth will anchor this change?

CLOSING REFLECTION

Ask participants to write down a one-sentence prayer expressing their desire for transformation in their morning routine.

MY ONE SENTENCE REQUEST

CLOSING PRAYER

Read together or select a volunteer.

Creator of morning, we thank You for the gift of each new day. As the sun rises on our world, may we rise to meet with You. Help us move beyond our reluctance and resistance to embrace the spiritual practice of morning prayer. May we, like the psalmist, lay our requests before You in the morning and wait expectantly. May we, like Jesus, seek solitude to hear Your voice before the demands of the day crowd in. We confess our need for the joy that comes in the morning—the renewal that can only be found in Your presence. Transform our mornings that our days might be transformed as well. In Jesus' name, amen.

INTRODUCTION

JOY COMES IN THE MORNING

PERSONAL BIBLE STUDY

DAY 1

THE LAMENT THAT LEADS TO HOPE

Begin by quieting your heart before God. Take three deep breaths, remembering that God's Spirit is with you in this moment.

CONTEXT SETTING

Today we will study one of Scripture's most profound passages about morning renewal. Written during the Babylonian exile after Jerusalem's destruction (586 BC), the book of Lamentations expresses Israel's deep grief. Yet even in this darkest moment, the prophet finds hope in God's faithfulness, particularly visible each morning.

Read: Lamentations 3:19–26

Inductive Study

1. **Observation:** What does the text say?

• Make a list of all the emotions and mental states the author expresses in verses 19–20.	
• In verse 21, identify the turning point in the passage. What specific phrase marks this shift?	
• In verses 22–23, list all the attributes of God that the author affirms.	
• What action does the author commit to in verse 24?	
• In verses 25–26, what does the author label as good?	

2. **Word Study: "Wait" (v. 24)** The Hebrew word translated "wait" is *qavah*, which carries the sense of hoping with eager expectation, like a taut rope under tension. This isn't passive waiting but active, expectant hope.

• How does understanding this word change your perception of what it means to wait for the Lord?	
• Look up Isaiah 40:31, which uses the same Hebrew word. How does this expand your understanding of waiting on God?	

3. **Cross-Reference Analysis:**

• Read Psalm 130:5–6, which uses the metaphor of watchmen waiting for morning. How does this complement the message in Lamentations?	
• Read Exodus 16:13–21 about the manna that appeared each morning. How does this historical example demonstrate God's daily faithfulness that Lamentations celebrates?	

4. **Interpretation:** What does the text mean?

• Why is remembering God's faithfulness crucial during times of suffering?	
• What theological significance is there in the author's assertion that God's mercies are "new every morning" (v. 23)?	
• How does the author's focus shift from his circumstances (vv. 19–20) to God's character (vv. 21–24)? What can we learn from this pattern?	

Theological Reflection

The author of Lamentations demonstrates a profound theological truth: Hope is not based on changing circumstances but on the unchanging character of God. Even in the midst of national catastrophe, the author anchors his hope in God's covenant faithfulness, which he observes renewed each morning. Morning becomes a daily reminder of God's commitment to His people, a tangible evidence of grace that doesn't depend on their faithfulness but on His character.

Personal Application

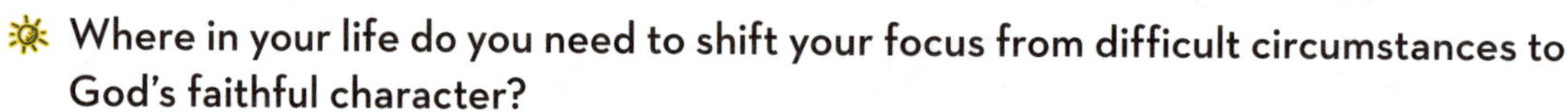

- Where in your life do you need to shift your focus from difficult circumstances to God's faithful character?

- How might beginning each day remembering God's mercies change your approach to challenges?

- What specific reminders can you place in your morning routine to help you recall God's faithfulness?

PRAYER

Lord, when my soul is downcast and I remember my affliction and wandering, help me to intentionally call to mind Your unfailing love. Thank You that Your compassions never fail but are new every morning. Great is Your faithfulness! Teach me to say with conviction that You are my portion, therefore I will hope in You. Help me to wait for You each morning with eager expectation. In Jesus' name, amen.

DAY 2
DAVID'S MORNING DISCIPLINE

Set aside distractions and focus your attention on God's presence with you now. Ask Him to open your heart to His Word.

CONTEXT SETTING

The Psalms give us intimate access to the prayer life of God's people, particularly David. As both warrior and worshiper, David understood the strategic importance of beginning the day with God, establishing morning prayer as a spiritual discipline long before the day's challenges arose.

Read: Psalm 5:1–8 (focusing especially on v. 3)

Inductive Study

1. Observation: What does the text say?

• What specific words does David use to describe his prayer in verses 1–2?	
• What attitude accompanies David's morning prayer according to verse 3?	
• How does David describe God's character in verses 4–6?	
• What action does David take in verse 7, and on what basis?	
• What request does David make in verse 8?	

2. Word Study: "Lay my requests" (v. 3) The Hebrew verb used here is *'arak* (אֶעֱרָךְ), meaning "to arrange" or "set in order." In Psalm 5:3, David says, "In the morning I prepare a sacrifice for you and watch" (ESV). The word can refer to arranging items for various purposes—sometimes in liturgical contexts, such as preparing the showbread in the tabernacle (Ex. 40:23), and other times in non-liturgical ones, such as arranging troops for battle (Judg. 20:20). The context of Psalm 5 suggests a deeply intentional act of worship.

• How does understanding David's use of the word *'arak* help you imagine prayer as more than spontaneous speech, but as something carefully and reverently laid before God?	
• What might it mean for your own prayer life to "arrange" your words before the Lord with such intentionality—like preparing an offering?	

3. Cross-Reference Analysis:

• Read Exodus 29:38–42, which describes the morning sacrifice in the tabernacle. How might David's morning prayer practice relate to this temple rhythm?	
• Read Daniel 6:10, noting Daniel's prayer routine. What similarities do you see with David's practice?	
• Read Mark 1:35. How did Jesus follow in this tradition of morning prayer?	

4. Interpretation: What does the text mean?

• Why do you think David emphasizes morning as his special time of prayer?	
• What is the significance of David saying he "waits expectantly" after prayer (v. 3)?	
• How does the surrounding context of this psalm (David's reflection on God's holiness and his enemies) inform our understanding of why morning prayer was important to him?	

Theological Reflection

David's morning prayer practice reveals a theological understanding that God deserves our first attention, not our leftover time. By "arranging" his prayers before God like a carefully prepared sacrifice, David shows that prayer is not casual but a deliberate, ordered communion with the holy God. His expectant waiting demonstrates faith that God not only hears but responds to prayer. For David, morning prayer wasn't merely about personal benefit but about aligning himself with God's character and ways before facing a world that often opposed both.

Personal Application

- What would it look like for you to "arrange" your prayers before God each morning rather than approaching prayer casually?

- How might waiting expectantly after prayer change your prayer experience?

- What practical steps can you take to establish morning prayer as a consistent discipline, following David's example?

PRAYER

God, hear my voice in the morning. Help me to deliberately arrange my prayers before You, not as hasty requests but as an offering of myself. Give me the discipline to rise and seek You first, and the faith to wait expectantly for Your response. Lead me in Your righteousness today, making Your way straight before me.In Jesus' name, amen.

DAY 3
JESUS' PRACTICE OF MORNING PRAYER

Begin with a moment of silence, acknowledging Christ's presence with you.

CONTEXT SETTING

Mark's Gospel portrays Jesus as constantly in motion, ministering to crowds with barely a moment's rest. Yet within this picture of constant activity, Mark reveals Jesus' secret to sustained ministry: withdrawal to solitary places for prayer, particularly in the early morning. Today's passage gives us a glimpse into Jesus' spiritual rhythms.

Read: Mark 1:29–39

Inductive Study

1. **Observation:** What does the text say?

Create a timeline of events in this passage, noting: • What happened at Simon's house (vv. 29–31) • What happened that evening (vv. 32–34) • What Jesus did "very early in the morning" (v. 35) • What happened after Simon found Jesus (vv. 36–39)	
• What specific details does Mark include about the timing and location of Jesus' prayer?	
• What interruption occurred during Jesus' prayer time?	
• What decision did Jesus make following His prayer time?	

2. **Structural Analysis:** Examine the structure of this passage, noting how Jesus' prayer time (v. 35) stands between two periods of intense ministry (vv. 29–34 and vv. 36–39). Consider how this structure might reveal the importance of prayer in Jesus' ministry.

3. **Cross-Reference Analysis:**

• Read Luke 5:15–16. What pattern do you notice in Jesus' prayer life?	
• Read Luke 6:12–13. What significant decision did Jesus make after a night of prayer?	
• Read Mark 6:45–46. In what way does this reinforce Jesus' pattern of seeking solitude for prayer?	
• Read Hebrews 5:7. How does this illuminate the nature of Jesus' prayers?	

4. **Interpretation:** What does the text mean?

• Why do you think Jesus chose to pray "very early in the morning, while it was still dark" (v. 35)?	
• What does Jesus' withdrawal for prayer reveal about His priorities?	
• What might we learn from Jesus' response to Simon's implied request to return to Capernaum?	
• How does Jesus' prayer life inform His sense of purpose and mission?	

Theological Reflection

Jesus' early morning prayer practice reveals profound theological truth about the incarnation. Though fully divine, the incarnate Christ depended on communion with the Father to fulfill His mission. His withdrawal for prayer wasn't an escape from ministry demands but was the very source of His power and clarity of purpose. The Son of God considered nothing—not sleep, popularity, or even legitimate ministry needs—more important than communion with the Father. This upends our tendency to view prayer as secondary to "real ministry" and shows that true spiritual power and direction flow from prayer, not activity.

Personal Application

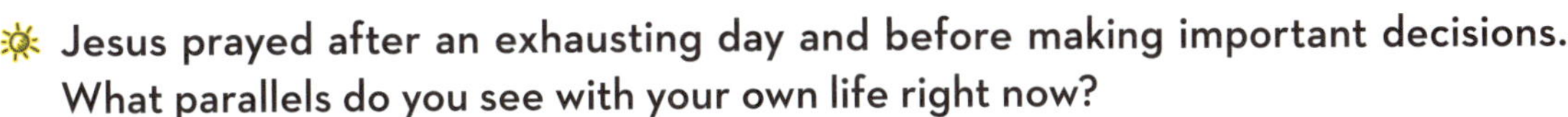

- **Jesus prayed after an exhausting day and before making important decisions. What parallels do you see with your own life right now?**

- **What "interruptions" typically disrupt your time with God? How can you respond to these with Jesus' sense of purpose?**

- **How would prioritizing prayer change your sense of purpose and ministry direction?**

- What practical adjustments would help you follow Jesus' example of solitary morning prayer?

PRAYER

Lord Jesus, thank You for modeling the priority of prayer even in the busiest seasons of ministry. Give me the discipline to rise early, seeking solitude with the Father before the demands of the day close in. Help me not to view prayer as an optional addition to ministry but as its essential foundation. Like You, may I emerge from prayer with clarity about God's calling on my life. In Jesus' name, amen.

DAY 4

MORNING PRAYER AS FOUNDATION FOR THE DAY

Quiet your heart before God, acknowledging your need for His guidance today.

CONTEXT SETTING

The psalmist of Psalm 143 writes from a place of distress, surrounded by enemies and feeling that his spirit is failing within him. Yet in the midst of this darkness, he turns to God in the morning, seeking direction and deliverance. This psalm reveals how morning prayer can anchor us even in life's most challenging seasons.

Read: Psalm 143:1–12 (focusing especially on vv. 5–10)

Inductive Study

1. Observation: What does the text say?

• What is the overall tone and emotional state of the psalmist in this prayer?	
• What past action does the psalmist recall in verse 5?	
• What physical gesture does the psalmist describe in verse 6, and what does this symbolize?	
• What specific request does the psalmist make regarding the morning in verse 8?	
• What reasons does the psalmist give for God to answer his prayer (vv. 8, 11–12)?	

2. Word Study: "Let the morning bring me word" (v. 8) The Hebrew phrase *hashmiʿēnî babōqer* can be rendered quite woodenly as "cause me to hear in the morning." This verb comes from a causative stem, indicating a plea for God to actively make His voice heard. While some translations, like the NIV, render it more gently as "let the morning bring me word," the original language underscores the depth of the request: David isn't just hoping to hear—he's asking God to *cause* him to hear.

• How does this deepen your understanding of morning prayer as a time not only for speaking to God but for listening with expectation?	
• What might it look like for you to begin each day with this plea: "God, cause me to hear Your unfailing love"?	

3. Cross-Reference Analysis:

• Read Exodus 16:4–8, noting when God provided manna. How does this connect with the concept of hearing from God in the morning?	
• Read Isaiah 50:4–5, where the Suffering Servant (prophetically pointing to Christ) speaks of God awakening his ear "morning by morning." What does this reveal about God's desire to communicate with us daily?	
• Read Psalm 90:14. How does this complement Psalm 143:8?	

4. Interpretation: What does the text mean?

• Why is hearing of God's unfailing love specifically in the morning significant?	
• How does the psalmist's request to know "the way I should go" (v. 8) relate to starting the day with God?	
• What connection exists between remembering God's past works (v. 5) and facing the current day?	
• How does entrusting one's life to God (v. 8) influence daily decisions and direction?	

Theological Reflection

Psalm 143 presents morning prayer not as a spiritual luxury but as essential spiritual orientation. The psalmist recognizes that without hearing of God's unfailing love at the day's beginning, he will struggle to navigate life's challenges. Morning becomes the critical moment when our souls must be anchored in God's covenant faithfulness before facing a world filled with enemies, trials, and temptations. This psalm also reveals the profound connection between remembering God's past works and finding courage for present challenges—a remembrance that happens most effectively when our minds are fresh at morning's dawn.

Personal Application

- **What would it mean for you to ask God to cause you to hear of His unfailing love each morning? How might this transform your day?**

- **The psalmist meditates on God's works and considers what His hands have done. How might you incorporate remembrance of God's faithfulness into your morning routine?**

- **In what specific area of your life do you need God to "show [you] the way [you] should go" (v. 8) right now?**

- Describe specifically how beginning your day seeking this guidance would change your approach to decisions.

PRAYER

Lord, cause me to hear of Your unfailing love in the morning, for I put my trust in You. Show me the way I should go today and every day, for to You I entrust my life. Like the psalmist, I spread out my hands to You; my soul thirsts for You like a parched land. Teach me to do Your will, for You are my God. May Your good Spirit lead me on level ground. For Your name's sake, O Lord, preserve my life. In Jesus' name, amen.

DAY 5

BEGINNING YOUR MORNING PRACTICE WITH STILLNESS

INTRODUCTION

This week, we begin our journey in contemplative prayer with a simple practice of morning stillness. This will become the foundation of your GREAT Morning Revolution—the first step in establishing a new pattern of beginning your day with God before anything else.

Read

"Be still, and know that I am God; I will be exalted among the nations, I will be exalted in the earth. The LORD Almighty is with us; the God of Jacob is our fortress."

Psalm 46:10–11

STARTING YOUR MORNING REVOLUTION

1. Claim Your Wake-Up Time: ______________________

- ☐ Decide when you'll begin your morning practice. I recommend setting your alarm 10–15 minutes earlier than your usual wake-up time.
- ☐ Set your alarm for this time every day for the next week.
- ☐ Place your alarm away from your bed so you have to physically get up to turn it off.

2. Create Your Sacred Space

- ☐ Designate a specific place for your morning practice—a comfortable chair, a corner of your bedroom, or any quiet space.
- ☐ Keep your Bible, journal, and this study guide in that space.
- ☐ Consider what might help you focus—perhaps a candle, a special mug for your morning beverage, or a cozy blanket.

MORNING STILLNESS PRACTICE

(10–15 MINUTES)

1. Begin with a few deep breaths. As you sit in quiet meditation, ask for God to align your heart with His.
2. Take a pen and piece of paper and acknowledge the presence of God that is there. Perhaps make a list of the ways that God is with you or the goodness of God in your life.
3. Slowly repeat Psalm 46:10, "Be still, and know that I am God."
4. Then gradually reduce the phrase, pausing between each iteration:
    - "Be still and know that I am God."
    - "Be still and know that I am."
    - "Be still and know."
    - "Be still."
    - "Be."
5. Rest in stillness for 5–7 minutes.

6. When thoughts arise (as they naturally will), gently return to your breath and the awareness of God's presence.
7. Slowly read Psalm 46:10–11 once more.
8. Close by praying the Lord's Prayer out loud or silently. If you're new to praying the Lord's Prayer, it's on page 185 in the study guide for your reference.

REFLECTION QUESTIONS

- What emotions or thoughts emerged during this time of stillness?
- How easy or difficult was it to be still? What made it challenging?
- How might beginning your day with stillness rather than immediately reaching for your phone or jumping into tasks change your approach to the day ahead?

YOUR WEEK 1 MORNING ROUTINE

For the coming week, commit to this simple practice of waking up 10–15 minutes earlier and spending time in stillness before God. Don't worry about doing it perfectly—just show up, day after day, creating the foundation for all that's to come.

PRAYER FOR THE WEEK AHEAD

Lord, thank You for the invitation to be still and know that You are God. As I begin this morning revolution, give me the discipline to rise and the desire to meet with You before meeting the demands of my day. Help me to create a new rhythm where stillness comes before activity and Your presence is my first priority. In Jesus' name, amen.

GRATITUDE

THE FOUNDATION OF MORNING PRAYER

(90 MINUTES)

WELCOME AND ICEBREAKER

(10 MINUTES)

For continuing groups, allow a few minutes for participants to reconnect.

Icebreaker: What is something small but significant you're grateful for today that you might typically overlook?

OPENING THEOLOGICAL REFLECTION

(5 MINUTES)

Select a volunteer to read aloud.

Gratitude stands at the center of the Christian life. From the earliest pages of Scripture, we're called to recognize that everything we have is a gift—that we live in a world we did not create, sustained by breath we did not generate, saved by grace we did not earn. The natural response to this realization is thanksgiving.

The biblical concept of gratitude goes beyond mere politeness or positive thinking. The Hebrew term for thanksgiving, *todah*, is connected to worship and sacrifice. To give thanks in Scripture is to acknowledge God's character, to declare His goodness not just in prosperous times but even in the valley of shadows (e.g., Pss. 30:12; 33:2; 44:8). One of the sacrifices was also called *todah*, the thank offering (e.g., Lev. 7:12; Ps. 116:17). The apostle Paul's command to "give thanks in all circumstances" (1 Thess. 5:18) isn't a call to superficial positivity but to a profound faith that recognizes God's faithfulness even when it's not immediately visible.

Morning gratitude, then, becomes a powerful theological act—a declaration that before we face the day's demands and challenges, we first acknowledge God as the Giver of all good gifts. It's an act of faith that frames our entire day in light of God's character rather than our circumstances.

As we explore gratitude as the foundation of morning prayer, we're entering into an ancient spiritual practice that has shaped believers through the centuries—a practice that doesn't deny life's difficulties but transforms how we experience them by first remembering God's goodness.

OPENING PRAYER

Pray together in unison or select a volunteer:

Generous God, we come before You recognizing that every good and perfect gift comes from Your hand. As we explore gratitude as the foundation of morning prayer, open our hearts to recognize Your presence and provision in our lives. Help us move beyond shallow thankfulness to a deeper gratitude rooted in who You are, not just what You do. May our gratitude become a powerful witness to Your goodness in a world that often focuses on scarcity rather than abundance. In Jesus' name, amen.

SCRIPTURE READING BEFORE TEACHING

Read Psalm 92:1–2 and 1 Thessalonians 5:16–18 aloud.

VIDEO TEACHING

(21 MINUTES)

Watch Week 2 video "Gratitude" streaming or on DVD.

NOTES

Use the space below to take notes if you'd like.

GROUP DISCUSSION

(45 MINUTES)

Leader, present each prompt, associated passages, and questions in order to the group. Where scripture is to be read, select a volunteer to read aloud to the group.

1. The Biblical Foundation of Gratitude

- Read Psalm 103:1–5. In this psalm, David begins with a call to his own soul to praise God, then lists specific reasons for gratitude. Why is it significant that David begins by commanding his own soul?

- How might this practice of deliberate gratitude apply to our morning routines?

2. Gratitude in All Circumstances

In 1 Thessalonians 5:18, Paul writes, "Give thanks in all circumstances; for this is God's will for you in Christ Jesus." The Greek preposition used here (*en*) means "in" not "for"—we are to give thanks *in* all circumstances, not necessarily *for* them.

- How does this distinction help us understand what biblical gratitude looks like during difficult seasons?

- Read Habakkuk 3:17–19. How does the prophet model gratitude in challenging circumstances?

- Share about a time when you were able to be grateful in the midst of difficulty. What made this possible?

3. Morning Gratitude as Spiritual Formation

Read Lamentations 3:22–23 and Psalm 92:1–2, which specifically mention morning as a time to declare God's love and faithfulness.

- What is the significance of beginning our day with gratitude rather than expressing it at other times?
- How might morning gratitude shape our perspective throughout the day?
- What physiological and psychological benefits of morning gratitude have you experienced?

4. From Entitlement to Gratitude

Read Deuteronomy 8:11–18, which warns against forgetting God when life is comfortable.

- How does our culture cultivate entitlement rather than gratitude?
- In what ways have you noticed entitlement creeping into your own spiritual life?
- What specific practices help move us from entitlement to gratitude?

5. Gratitude as Witness

Read Philippians 2:14–16, where Paul connects the absence of complaining with shining like stars in the world.

- How does gratitude serve as a countercultural witness in today's world?

- In what settings do you find it most challenging to maintain a grateful spirit?

- How might beginning your day with gratitude influence your witness in these challenging environments?

6. Gratitude for God's Work

Read Luke 17:11–17, where Jesus heals ten men of leprosy but only one thanks Him.

- Why do you think only one man returned to thank Jesus?

- What might be the significance of the one who returned being a Samaritan, a foreigner?

- How can you remember to praise God and thank Jesus for answered requests?

7. Practical Steps Toward Morning Gratitude

- What specific elements could you incorporate into your morning routine to cultivate gratitude?

- What obstacles might you face in establishing this practice, and how will you address them?

- How might technology either help or hinder your practice of morning gratitude?

CLOSING REFLECTION

Ask participants to complete this sentence in writing.

MY ONE SENTENCE REQUEST

I want to begin my mornings with gratitude because . . .

CLOSING PRAYER

Read together or select a volunteer.

Gracious God, we thank You for Your countless gifts—for life and breath, for love and connection, for Your presence that never leaves us. Forgive us for the times we've taken Your goodness for granted or allowed complaints to drown out thanksgiving. As we go from this place, help us to notice Your gifts with fresh eyes. May gratitude be our first response when we wake, shaping our thoughts, our words, and our actions throughout the day. Teach us the discipline of giving thanks, not just when life is good, but in all circumstances, trusting Your faithful love. In Jesus' name, amen.

THE FOUNDATION OF MORNING PRAYER

PERSONAL BIBLE STUDY

DAY 1

THE COMMAND TO GIVE THANKS

Begin by centering your heart on God's presence, remembering that gratitude begins with awareness of the Giver.

CONTEXT SETTING

Paul's first letter to the Thessalonians was written to encourage a young church facing persecution. Amid instructions about community life, Paul offers three short commands that have profound implications for spiritual formation: Rejoice always, pray continually, and give thanks in all circumstances. Today we'll explore why thanksgiving isn't optional but essential to Christian faith.

Read: 1 Thessalonians 5:16–18

Inductive Study

1. Observation: What does the text say?

• List the three commands Paul gives in these verses.	
• What qualifier does Paul attach to each command?	
• What reason does Paul give for these commands in verse 18?	
• How are these three commands related to each other?	

2. **Word Study: "Give thanks" (v. 18)** The Greek word for "give thanks" is *eucharisteō*, from which we get "Eucharist." In Greek culture, this term was used for expressing gratitude to the gods or to benefactors. In Christian usage, it took on deeper meaning as recognition of God's grace (*charis*).

• How does understanding this word's connection to grace (*charis*) deepen your understanding of thanksgiving?	
• Look up Colossians 3:15–17. The adjective *eucharistos* is used in verse 15; the noun *charis* is used in verse 15; the verb *eucharisteō* is used in verse 17. What insights does this repetition offer about the centrality of thanksgiving?	

3. **Cross-Reference Analysis:**

• Read Ephesians 5:20. How does this parallel passage expand our understanding of thanksgiving?	
• Read Hebrews 13:15. How does this verse describe thanksgiving as a sacrifice?	
• Read Psalm 50:23. What does this verse suggest about the spiritual significance of thanksgiving?	

4. Interpretation: What does the text mean?

• Why might Paul link these three commands (rejoice, pray, give thanks) together?	
• What does it mean that giving thanks is "God's will for you in Christ Jesus" (v. 18)?	
• How can we genuinely give thanks "in all circumstances" (v. 18), including difficult ones?	
• What is the difference between giving thanks *for* all circumstances and *in* all circumstances?	

Theological Reflection

Paul's command to "give thanks in all circumstances" (v. 18) reveals that gratitude is not meant to be an occasional response to blessing but a fundamental orientation of the Christian life. By declaring this to be "God's will for you in Christ Jesus" (v. 18), Paul elevates thanksgiving from a social nicety to a central aspect of our identity as believers. This command challenges the assumption that gratitude should follow only from favorable circumstances. Instead, thanksgiving becomes an act of faith—a declaration that God remains good and trustworthy even when life is difficult. Morning thanksgiving, then, becomes a powerful way to orient ourselves to this divine reality before facing the day's challenges.

Personal Application

☼ **Reflect on a current challenging circumstance in your life. How might you practice giving thanks in (not necessarily for) this situation?**

- Consider how beginning your day with deliberate thanksgiving might change your approach to difficulties you're facing. Write your thoughts in the space below.

- What specific aspects of God's character can you thank Him for each morning, regardless of your circumstances?

PRAYER

Faithful God, I confess that giving thanks in all circumstances is challenging. Help me to develop a heart of gratitude that isn't dependent on favorable conditions but on Your unchanging character. As I begin each morning, teach me to thank You before I face the day's challenges, knowing that Your goodness transcends my circumstances. May thanksgiving become as natural as breathing, shaping how I view every aspect of my life. In Jesus' name, amen.

DAY 2

MORNING DECLARATION OF GOD'S GOODNESS

Take a moment to acknowledge God's presence, opening yourself to receive His goodness.

CONTEXT SETTING

Psalm 92 is designated in the NIV as "A psalm. A song. For the Sabbath day." It was likely used in temple worship, inviting worshipers to begin their day of rest with declarations of God's goodness. The psalm connects morning with gratitude, establishing a pattern that shapes not just one day but an entire life of worship.

Read: Psalm 92:1–15 (focusing especially on vv. 1–5)

Inductive Study

1. **Observation:** What does the text say?

• What two times of day does the psalmist specifically mention for giving thanks?	
• What musical instruments does the psalmist mention in verses 1–3?	
• What reason does the psalmist give for praising God in verse 4?	
• What contrasting responses to God's works are described in verses 5–6?	
• What imagery does the psalmist use in verses 12–14 to describe the righteous?	

2. **Word Study: "Proclaim" (v. 2)** The Hebrew word translated "proclaim" is *nagad*, which means "to declare, tell, or announce." It carries the sense of making something known publicly rather than keeping it private.

• How does this understanding challenge our concept of gratitude as merely a private feeling?	
• What significance is there in publicly declaring God's love and faithfulness?	

3. **Cross-Reference Analysis:**

• Read Psalm 59:16. How does this verse similarly connect morning with declarations of God's character?	
• Read Psalm 143:8. What does the psalmist ask to hear in the morning?	
• Read Exodus 16:13–21. How does God's provision of morning manna relate to the theme of declaring God's faithfulness at daybreak?	

4. Interpretation: What does the text mean?

• Why does the psalmist highlight both morning and night as times to proclaim God's attributes?	
• What connection exists between thankfulness and the ability to perceive God's works (vv. 4–6)?	
• How does beginning the day with gratitude prepare us to face the reality that "the wicked spring up like grass" (v. 7)?	
• What does the flourishing described in verses 12–14 suggest about the long-term effects of a life rooted in gratitude?	

Theological Reflection

Psalm 92 reveals that morning gratitude is more than a spiritual technique—it's a profound theological declaration that frames our entire day. By beginning with thanksgiving, we establish God's goodness as the foundation from which we interpret all of life's events. The contrast between those who perceive God's wondrous deeds (vv. 4–5) and those who cannot understand (v. 6) suggests that gratitude actually shapes our spiritual perception. The flourishing described at the psalm's conclusion portrays gratitude not as a momentary practice but as a lifelong orientation that produces enduring spiritual vitality. Morning thanksgiving becomes a kind of spiritual root system, drawing nourishment from God's faithfulness and producing fruit even in old age.

Personal Application

☼ **Consider how you might incorporate both morning and evening thanksgiving into your daily routine. What difference might this "bookending" make?**

- The psalmist uses musical instruments in praise. How might you creatively express gratitude beyond just words?

- Is there a specific work of God in your life that fills you with gladness? How can you make this the focus of your morning gratitude?

- What would it look like for you to proclaim God's love and faithfulness rather than simply feel grateful for them?

PRAYER

Lord, it is good to give thanks to You, to sing praises to Your name, O Most High. Help me to proclaim Your unfailing love in the morning and Your faithfulness at night. Fill my heart with such gladness at Your works that I cannot help but sing for joy. May my life be like a flourishing palm tree or cedar of Lebanon—rooted in gratitude, bearing fruit even in old age, proclaiming that You are my rock and there is no unrighteousness in You. In Jesus' name, amen.

DAY 3

GRATITUDE THAT OVERCOMES ANXIETY

Begin with a moment of stillness, releasing your anxieties and opening yourself to God's peace.

CONTEXT SETTING

Paul's letter to the Philippians was written from prison, yet it overflows with joy and gratitude. In today's passage, Paul provides practical guidance for dealing with anxiety through thanksgiving. This teaching reveals the transformative power of gratitude not just as an emotion but as a spiritual practice that guards our hearts and minds.

Read: Philippians 4:4–9

Inductive Study

1. **Observation:** What does the text say?

• What repeated command does Paul give in verse 4?	
• What character quality does Paul urge believers to display in verse 5, and why?	
• What specific instruction about anxiety does Paul give in verse 6?	
• What does Paul say will be the result of prayer with thanksgiving in verse 7?	
• What are believers instructed to think about in verse 8?	
• What promise does Paul make in verse 9 to those who practice these things?	

2. **Word Study: "With thanksgiving" (v. 6)** The Greek phrase *meta eucharistias* literally means "accompanied by thanksgiving." The preposition *meta* indicates association or accompaniment, suggesting that thanksgiving should be the constant companion of our prayers.

• How does this phrase modify our understanding of how to present requests to God?	
• What attitude does this suggest should accompany even our most urgent petitions?	

3. **Cross-Reference Analysis:**

• Read Colossians 4:2. How does this verse similarly connect watchfulness in prayer with thanksgiving?	
• Read 1 Timothy 2:1–2. What place does thanksgiving have in relation to various types of prayers?	
• Read Hebrews 12:28. How does this verse connect thanksgiving with acceptable worship?	

4. Interpretation: What does the text mean?

• Why does Paul place thanksgiving in the context of anxiety?	
• What does it mean that God's peace will "guard your hearts and your minds" (v. 7)?	
• How does the command to rejoice (v. 4) relate to prayer with thanksgiving (v. 6)?	
• What connection exists between gratitude (v. 6) and thought life (v. 8)?	

Theological Reflection

Paul's instruction reveals gratitude as a powerful spiritual antidote to anxiety. By coupling prayer with thanksgiving, we affirm God's goodness and sovereignty even before receiving answers to our petitions. This isn't mere positive thinking but a theological declaration that God is trustworthy regardless of circumstances. The peace that guards our hearts and minds isn't simply emotional calm but a divine sentinel—the very peace of God that surpasses understanding—protecting us from anxiety's assault. Morning gratitude, then, becomes a preemptive spiritual practice, establishing a foundation of peace before the day's worries arise. By beginning with thanksgiving, we create a mental and spiritual environment where anxiety struggles to take root.

Personal Application

☼ **Identify specific anxieties that tend to dominate your thoughts. How might beginning your day with thanksgiving for God's faithfulness change your approach to these concerns?**

- Paul instructs us to present our requests "with thanksgiving" (v. 6). What might this look like in your prayer life?

- Consider how the practice of morning gratitude might help establish the thought patterns described in verse 8 (whatever is true, noble, right, pure, lovely, admirable).

- What specific truths about God's character could you thank Him for each morning that would help combat your particular anxieties?

PRAYER

Lord, I rejoice in You always. Instead of being anxious, I present my requests to You with thanksgiving, trusting that Your peace—which transcends all understanding—will guard my heart and mind in Christ Jesus. Help me to focus my thoughts on whatever is true, noble, right, pure, lovely, admirable, excellent, and praiseworthy. As I begin each day with gratitude, establish Your peace as the foundation of my day. In Jesus' name, amen.

DAY 4

INGRATITUDE AND ITS CONSEQUENCES

Begin by asking God to open your heart to His Word, even when it challenges you.

CONTEXT SETTING

Romans 1 contains one of Paul's most profound theological analyses of human sin. Surprisingly, he identifies ingratitude—failure to give thanks—as a pivotal step in humanity's downward spiral away from God. Today we'll explore why ingratitude is not merely impolite but spiritually devastating, providing insight into why morning gratitude is essential for spiritual health.

Read: Romans 1:18–25

Inductive Study

1. **Observation:** What does the text say?

• According to verse 19, what has been made known to all people?	
• What does verse 20 say is revealed through creation?	
• What two responses did people fail to have toward God (v. 21)?	
• What happened to people's thinking as a result (vv. 21–22)?	
• What did people worship instead of the Creator (vv. 23, 25)?	
• What was God's response to this rejection (v. 24)?	

2. Word Study: "Neither glorified . . . nor gave thanks" (v. 21) The Greek word for "gave thanks" is *eucharistēsan* (from *eucharisteō*). When paired with "glorified" (*edoxasan*), it suggests that gratitude is intrinsically connected to giving God proper honor and recognition.

• How does this pairing of glorifying and thanking illuminate the theological significance of gratitude?	
• What does this suggest about ingratitude as more than just bad manners?	

3. Cross-Reference Analysis:

• Read Deuteronomy 8:10–18. What warning does Moses give about forgetting God in the midst of prosperity?	
• Read 2 Timothy 3:1–5. How is ingratitude connected to other characteristics of godlessness in the last days?	
• Read Luke 17:11–19. What does Jesus' response to the one thankful leper reveal about the importance of gratitude?	

4. Interpretation: What does the text mean?

• Why does Paul place ingratitude at such a pivotal position in humanity's rejection of God?	
• What is the connection between ingratitude and the darkening of the human mind (v. 21)?	
• How does failure to give thanks lead to idolatry (vv. 23, 25)?	
• What does this passage reveal about gratitude as essential to proper relationship with God?	

Theological Reflection

Romans 1 reveals the profound theological significance of gratitude. Far from being a peripheral virtue, thanksgiving is foundational to right relationship with God. Ingratitude represents a refusal to acknowledge our dependency as creatures, leading to the self-deception that we are self-sufficient. This delusion inevitably results in idolatry—the worship of created things rather than the Creator. Morning gratitude, then, isn't simply a positive practice but a vital spiritual discipline that daily reorients us to reality: We are dependent creatures, and everything we have is a gift. By beginning each day with thanksgiving, we counteract the darkening effect of ingratitude on our minds and guard against the idolatry that follows when we fail to acknowledge God as the source of all good gifts.

Personal Application

☼ **Consider areas where you might be taking God's gifts for granted. How might deliberate morning gratitude for these gifts reorient your heart?**

- In what ways has ingratitude led to "darkened" thinking in your own life or in the broader culture (v. 21)?

- Identify potential "created things" (v. 25) that you might be tempted to worship instead of the Creator. How could morning thanksgiving help guard against this tendency?

- What specific aspects of God's "eternal power and divine nature" (v. 20) seen in creation could you incorporate into your morning gratitude practice?

PRAYER

Creator God, forgive me for the times I have neither glorified You as God nor given You thanks. I acknowledge that every good gift comes from Your hand. Guard my heart against the spiritual darkness that comes from ingratitude. Help me to begin each day recognizing and thanking You for Your eternal power and divine nature revealed in creation, and for Your grace revealed in salvation. May thanksgiving protect me from the idolatry of worshiping created things rather than You, the eternal Creator. In Jesus' name, amen.

DAY 5

ADDING GRATITUDE TO YOUR MORNING ROUTINE

INTRODUCTION

This week, we build on our foundation of morning stillness by adding the practice of gratitude. Gratitude is a powerful way to notice God's gifts and to begin each day with thanksgiving. This becomes the second element of your GREAT Morning Revolution.

Read

Let the peace of Christ rule in your hearts, since as members of one body you were called to peace. And be thankful. Let the message of Christ dwell among you richly as you teach and admonish one another with all wisdom through psalms, hymns, and songs from the Spirit, singing to God with gratitude in your hearts. And whatever you do, whether in word or deed, do it all in the name of the Lord Jesus, giving thanks to God the Father through him.

Colossians 3:15–17

EXPANDING YOUR MORNING REVOLUTION

1. Morning Stillness (5–7 minutes)

- Begin with your established practice of stillness.
- Take several deep breaths, becoming aware of God's presence.
- Repeat "Be still, and know that I am God" (Ps. 46:10), gradually reducing the phrase.
- Rest in God's presence for a few minutes.

2. Morning Gratitude (10–12 minutes)

- Transition to gratitude with a simple prayer: "Lord, open my eyes to see Your gifts in my life."
- Review the previous day, noting moments of blessing:
  - A kind word or gesture
  - A moment of beauty
  - A challenge overcome
  - An unexpected provision
  - A relationship that sustains you
- As each gift comes to mind, offer a simple "thank you."
- Write down 3–5 things you're grateful for in your journal.
- Consider how beginning your day with gratitude might shift your perspective on challenges ahead.

3. Closing in Thankfulness (3–5 minutes)

- Read Psalm 103:1–5 as your prayer of thanksgiving.
- Or offer your own prayer of gratitude, expressing thanks for specific gifts.
- Ask God to help you maintain an attitude of thankfulness throughout the day.
- Close by praying the Lord's Prayer out loud or silently (found on page 185).

REFLECTION QUESTIONS

What surprised you about this practice of morning gratitude?

Did you notice any resistance within yourself to acknowledging gifts? What might this reveal?

☀ **How does beginning your day with gratitude shift your perspective on the day ahead?**

YOUR WEEK 2 MORNING ROUTINE

For the coming week, commit to waking up early enough to practice both stillness (5–7 minutes) and gratitude (10–12 minutes) before facing the day's demands. You might need to set your alarm 5–10 minutes earlier than last week to accommodate this expanded practice.

PRAYER FOR THE WEEK AHEAD

Gracious God, thank You for Your countless gifts—seen and unseen, recognized and overlooked. As I add gratitude to my morning practice, cultivate in me a heart that notices Your goodness in all things. Help me to begin each day by declaring Your faithfulness, thanking You not only for what You give but for whom You are. May gratitude become the foundation of my life, shaping how I see the world and respond to both blessings and challenges. In Jesus' name, amen.

REFLECT

LOOKING WITHIN
AND LOOKING BACK

(90 MINUTES)

WELCOME AND ICEBREAKER

(10 MINUTES)

For continuing groups, allow a few minutes for participants to reconnect.

Icebreaker: What's one insight you've gained about yourself in the past year that has helped you grow spiritually?

OPENING THEOLOGICAL REFLECTION

(5 MINUTES)

Select a volunteer to read aloud.

In a culture of constant distraction and forward motion, the spiritual discipline of reflection offers a powerful countercultural practice. Scripture repeatedly calls God's people to remember, to consider, to examine—to pause and look both inward and backward. Psalms is filled with the language of reflection: "I remember the days of long ago; I meditate on all your works" (Ps. 143:5); "Search me, God, and know my heart" (Ps. 139:23).

This practice of reflection isn't merely psychological introspection but a theologically rich engagement with God's presence and action in our lives. When we reflect, we participate in God's own knowing of us. As Augustine prayed, "Grant, Lord, that I may know myself that I may know Thee." Self-knowledge and knowledge of God are intimately connected.

The morning offers a unique opportunity for this sacred reflection—a quiet space before the day's demands to look honestly at ourselves, to remember God's faithfulness, and to reorient our hearts toward His purposes. This isn't about dwelling in the past or becoming overly introspective but about allowing God's Spirit to illuminate our lives with His truth, preparing us to move forward with greater wisdom and self-awareness.

As we explore reflection as an essential element of morning prayer, we enter a practice that transforms not just our days but our very selves—a practice that opens us to the Spirit's work of conviction, healing, and renewal.

OPENING PRAYER

Pray together in unison or select a volunteer:

God who searches hearts and knows all things, we come before You acknowledging that we often rush through life without the gift of reflection. As we explore this essential practice, give us courage to look honestly at ourselves and wisdom to recognize Your faithful presence in our stories. May this time of study deepen our capacity for self-awareness and our appreciation of Your unfolding work in our lives. Help us to embrace reflection not as mere introspection but as sacred space for transformation. In Jesus' name, amen.

SCRIPTURE READING BEFORE TEACHING

Read Psalm 139:23–24 and Lamentations 3:40 aloud.

VIDEO TEACHING

(26 MINUTES)

Watch Week 3 video "Reflect" streaming or on DVD.

NOTES

Use the space below to take notes if you'd like.

GROUP DISCUSSION

(45 MINUTES)

Leader, present each prompt, associated passages, and questions in order to the group. Where scripture is to be read, select a volunteer to read aloud to the group.

1. Biblical Models of Reflection

Read Psalm 77:1–12. Notice how the psalmist moves from distress to confidence through the practice of reflection.

- What triggers the psalmist's reflection in this passage?
- How does the deliberate choice to remember God's past works change the psalmist's perspective?
- What can we learn from this pattern of moving from personal distress to remembered faithfulness?

2. Self-Examination as Spiritual Discipline

Read 2 Corinthians 13:5 and 1 Corinthians 11:28–32, where Paul calls believers to examine themselves.

- What is the difference between healthy self-examination and unhealthy introspection?
- How does the gospel provide the proper foundation for looking honestly at ourselves?
- What role does the Holy Spirit play in the practice of self-examination?

3. The Morning as Sacred Time for Reflection

Read Psalm 5:3 and Psalm 143:8, which specifically mention morning as a time to seek God.

- Why might morning be particularly suitable for the practice of reflection?

- What benefits have you experienced from reflecting in the morning rather than at other times?

- What practical challenges arise when trying to establish a morning reflection practice?

4. Reflection on God's Word

Read Psalm 119:15–16 and James 1:22–25, which speak of meditating on and reflecting on God's Word.

- How does Scripture provide a lens for healthy self-reflection?

- What is the connection between reflecting on Scripture and reflecting on our lives?

- How might morning reflection on Scripture shape your approach to the day ahead?

5. Remembering God's Faithfulness

Read Joshua 4:1–7, where God commands the Israelites to create a memorial of stones to prompt future reflection.

- Why is remembering God's past faithfulness so important for present faith?

- What "stones of remembrance" have you established to help you recall God's work in your life?

- How might deliberate reflection on God's past faithfulness strengthen you for current challenges?

6. The Examen as a Reflection Practice

The Prayer of Examen is an ancient spiritual practice that involves reflecting on where God has been present in our day. It includes gratitude, review, awareness of emotions, confession, and looking forward.

- How might adapting the Examen for morning prayer help you notice God's presence more intentionally?

- What elements of the Examen listed above seem most valuable for your spiritual growth right now?

- How does the practice of regular reflection foster spiritual growth over time?

7. From Reflection to Action

Read James 1:22–25 again, noting the connection between reflection and action.

- How does morning reflection prepare us for faithful action throughout the day?

- What is the danger of reflection without corresponding action?

- How might your day be different if you began with intentional reflection?

CLOSING REFLECTION

Ask participants to complete this sentence in writing.

MY ONE SENTENCE REQUEST

Through the practice of morning reflection, I hope to . . .

CLOSING PRAYER

Read together or select a volunteer.

Searching God, we thank You for the gift of reflection—for the invitation to pause and notice Your presence in our lives. Give us courage to look honestly at ourselves, without shame or pretense, trusting in Your grace that covers all. Help us to remember Your faithfulness in the past, that we might face the future with confidence. As we develop the practice of morning reflection, may our self-awareness deepen and our sensitivity to Your Spirit increase. Guide us to move from reflection to faithful action, that our lives might more fully reflect Your love and truth. In Jesus' name, amen.

LOOKING WITHIN
AND LOOKING BACK

PERSONAL BIBLE STUDY

DAY 1

THE CALL TO SELF-EXAMINATION

Begin by quieting your heart before God, inviting His searching presence.

CONTEXT SETTING

Psalm 139 offers one of Scripture's most profound invitations to self-examination. Unlike secular introspection, which can become self-absorbed, biblical self-examination always occurs in the context of God's loving presence. The psalmist recognizes that true self-knowledge comes through God's all-knowing gaze. Today, we'll explore how inviting God's searching presence becomes the foundation for morning reflection.

Read: Psalm 139:1–24

Inductive Study

1. **Observation:** What does the text say?

• What aspects of the psalmist's life does God know according to verses 1–6?	
• Where can the psalmist go to escape God's presence according to verses 7–12?	
• What does the psalmist acknowledge about God's role in his formation in verses 13–16?	
• How does the psalmist respond to God's thoughts in verses 17–18?	
• What request does the psalmist make in verses 23–24?	

2. Word Study: "Search" and "Know" (vv. 1, 23) The Hebrew word translated "search" (*khaqar*) means "to examine thoroughly," "to investigate," or "to search out." It suggests careful, deliberate examination rather than casual observation. "Know" (*yada*) refers to intimate, experiential knowledge, not just intellectual awareness.

• How does understanding these words deepen your appreciation of what the psalmist is asking?	
• What does it reveal about the depth of self-examination the psalmist is inviting?	

3. Cross-Reference Analysis:

• Read Jeremiah 17:9–10. How does this passage complement Psalm 139's perspective on self-knowledge?	
• Read 1 Corinthians 4:3–5. How does Paul's attitude toward self-judgment relate to the psalmist's approach?	
• Read Hebrews 4:12–13. What role does God's Word play in the process of self-examination?	

4. Interpretation: What does the text mean?

• Why does the psalmist begin with God's complete knowledge of him before asking God to search him?	
• What is the significance of the prayer "know my heart" (v. 23) when God already knows everything?	
• How does the psalmist's request for God to "lead me in the way everlasting" (v. 24) relate to self-examination?	
• What is the purpose of divine searching according to this psalm?	

Theological Reflection

Psalm 139 reveals that true self-knowledge is impossible apart from God's searching presence. The psalmist recognizes that we cannot see ourselves clearly through our own efforts; we need divine illumination. This fundamentally reframes the practice of morning reflection from self-focused introspection to God-centered examination. When we invite God to search us and know us, we acknowledge that His perspective of our lives is clearer than our own. The goal of this searching is not shame or self-improvement but guidance in "the way everlasting"—a life aligned with God's purposes (v. 24). Morning reflection becomes a sacred space where we submit ourselves to God's loving gaze, allowing Him to reveal what we cannot see on our own.

Personal Application

☼ **What aspects of your life might you be blind to that God sees clearly?**

- How might beginning your day by inviting God's searching presence change your approach to self-awareness?

- What fears or resistances do you experience when considering God's thorough knowledge of you?

- How could you incorporate the prayer "Search me, God, and know my heart" into your morning routine (v. 23)?

PRAYER

O Lord, You have searched me, and You know me. You know when I sit and when I rise; You perceive my thoughts from afar. You are familiar with all my ways. Before a word is on my tongue, You know it completely. Such knowledge is too wonderful for me, too lofty for me to attain. Search me, O God, and know my heart today; test me and know my anxious thoughts. See if there is any offensive way in me, and lead me in the way everlasting. I invite Your searching presence as I begin this day. In Jesus' name, amen.

DAY 2

REMEMBERING GOD'S WORKS

Begin by stilling your heart, creating space to remember God's faithfulness.

CONTEXT SETTING

Psalm 77 captures the journey from despair to hope through the practice of remembering God's works. The psalmist begins in deep distress, crying out to God without finding comfort. But a dramatic shift occurs when he deliberately chooses to remember God's past faithfulness. This psalm offers a powerful model for how morning reflection on God's works can transform our perspective on present challenges.

Read: Psalm 77:1–20

Inductive Study

1. Observation: What does the text say?

• Describe the psalmist's emotional state in verses 1–9. What phrases indicate his distress?	
• What questions does the psalmist ask in verses 7–9?	
• What specific works of God does the psalmist remember in verses 11–20?	
• How does the tone change from the beginning to the end of the psalm?	

2. Word Study: "Remember" and "Meditate" (vv. 11–12) The Hebrew word for "remember" (*zakar*) can include more than mental recall; it suggests bringing to mind the past in the present with such force that it shapes one's actions. "Meditate" (*hagah*) implies focusing thought, muttering or speaking quietly, and dwelling deeply on something.

• How does understanding these words expand your concept of remembering God's works?	
• What does this suggest about the active, intentional nature of biblical remembrance?	

3. Cross-Reference Analysis:

• Read Deuteronomy 8:2–5. What connection does Moses make between remembering and obedience?	
• Read Joshua 4:4–7. How did God institutionalize remembrance for Israel?	
• Read Psalm 143:5–6. How does this parallel passage connect remembrance with present spiritual thirst?	

4. Interpretation: What does the text mean?

• Why was remembering God's past work the turning point for the psalmist's distress?	
• What significance is there in the psalmist's focus on the exodus and Red Sea crossing?	
• How does remembering God's mighty deeds address the questions raised in verses 7–9?	
• What is the theological connection between memory and hope in this psalm?	

Theological Reflection

Psalm 77 reveals remembrance as a powerful spiritual practice that transforms our perspective on present suffering. The psalmist demonstrates that spiritual amnesia—forgetting God's past faithfulness—can lead to despair and doubt. But deliberate remembrance of God's mighty acts reorients our faith. This isn't mere nostalgia but a theological declaration that the God who acted powerfully in the past is still at work. Morning reflection on God's faithfulness becomes a vital spiritual discipline that anchors us in truth before facing the day's challenges. By remembering who God is and what He has done, we gain strength and perspective for whatever difficulties lie ahead.

Personal Application

☼ **What current challenges are causing you to question God's presence or goodness, as the psalmist did?**

- What specific works of God in your own life could you intentionally remember each morning?

- How might creating a regular practice of remembering God's faithfulness change your approach to difficulties?

- What practical method could you use to record and revisit evidence of God's work in your life?

PRAYER

Lord, when my soul refuses comfort and my spirit is overwhelmed, help me to remember Your deeds and meditate on all Your works. Like the psalmist, I choose to recall Your wonders of old and consider all Your mighty acts. You are the God who does wonders, who has displayed Your strength among the peoples. Your way is holy—who is great like You? As I begin this day, I remember how You have led Your people like a flock, how You have guided me through waters deep and trials fierce. Strengthen my faith through remembrance of Your faithfulness. In Jesus' name, amen.

DAY 3
REFLECTION FOR REPENTANCE

Begin by acknowledging God's presence, inviting His gentle conviction.

CONTEXT SETTING

Lamentations was written after Jerusalem's destruction by Babylon—Israel's darkest hour. Yet in this book of grief, we find one of Scripture's most powerful calls to reflection. The author recognizes that returning to God must begin with honest examination of one's ways. Today, we'll explore how morning reflection becomes a pathway to repentance and renewed relationship with God.

Read: Lamentations 3:37–42

Inductive Study

1. **Observation:** What does the text say?

• What theological truth does the author establish in verses 37–38?	
• What question does the author ask in verse 39?	
• What specific action does the author call for in verse 40?	
• What should follow the examination of one's ways according to verses 40–41?	
• To whom should hearts and hands be lifted?	

2. **Word Study: "Examine" and "Test" (v. 40)** The Hebrew word for "examine" (*khaphas*) means to search out carefully or investigate thoroughly. It suggests not a casual glance but a deliberate inspection. "Test" (*chaqar*) means to explore or search, often implying penetrating to the very core of something.

• How do these word meanings enhance your understanding of the reflection called for?	
• What does this suggest about the depth and honesty required in spiritual self-examination?	

3. **Cross-Reference Analysis:**

• Read 2 Corinthians 13:5. How does Paul's instruction to examine oneself echo Lamentations 3:40?	
• Read 1 Corinthians 11:28–32. What connection does Paul make between self-examination and divine discipline?	
• Read Haggai 1:5–7. What areas of life does God call His people to examine?	

4. Interpretation: What does the text mean?

• Why does the author establish God's sovereignty (vv. 37–38) before calling for self-examination?	
• What is the relationship between examining one's ways and returning to the Lord?	
• How does lifting "hearts and ... hands" (v. 41) to God relate to the process of examination and repentance?	
• What role does honest reflection play in spiritual renewal according to this passage?	

Theological Reflection

Lamentations 3:40 reveals reflection as essential to authentic repentance. Simply feeling sorry for sin isn't sufficient; God calls us to carefully examine our ways and test them against His truth. This practice occurs in the context of God's sovereignty (vv. 37–38), reminding us that our reflection isn't merely psychological introspection but submission to divine authority. The progression from examination to returning to the Lord demonstrates that true reflection always leads us back to God. Morning reflection becomes a sacred time to honestly assess our lives—not to wallow in guilt but to lift our hearts and hands to God in surrender and renewed commitment. In a culture that often avoids honest self-assessment, this practice becomes countercultural and transformative.

Personal Application

☼ **What areas of your life might need honest examination in light of God's Word?**

- How could beginning your day with reflective self-examination change your awareness of sin and need for grace?

- What is the difference between reflection that leads to shame and reflection that leads to returning to God?

- What specific practice could help you "examine [y]our ways and test them" (v. 40) as part of your morning routine?

PRAYER

Lord, I heed Your call to examine and test my ways and return to You. Give me courage to look honestly at my life, to see what You see without defensiveness or excuse. Guard me from both self-condemnation and self-justification. As I reflect on my ways, draw me back to Your unfailing love and mercy. I lift my heart and hands to You, O God in heaven, acknowledging my need for Your forgiveness and grace. May my morning reflection lead not to despair but to deeper communion with You. In Jesus' name, amen.

DAY 4
REFLECTION ON GOD'S WORD

Begin by stilling your mind and heart, creating space to receive God's Word.

CONTEXT SETTING

James offers one of Scripture's most powerful images for biblical reflection—looking intently into God's perfect law as into a mirror. Unlike casual glances that are quickly forgotten, the kind of reflection James describes changes how we live. Today we'll explore how morning meditation on Scripture becomes transformative reflection, shaping our actions throughout the day.

Read: James 1:19–25

Inductive Study

1. **Observation:** What does the text say?

• What command does James give about listening and speaking in verse 19?	
• What does human anger not produce according to verse 20?	
• What metaphor does James use for God's Word in verses 23–24?	
• What contrasting responses to God's Word does James describe?	
• What result comes from the right kind of reflection according to verse 25?	

2. Word Study: "Looks intently" (v. 25) The Greek word for "looks intently" (*parakyptō*) means "to stoop down or lean forward," "to peer into something with careful scrutiny." It suggests not a casual glance but concentrated attention and focus.

• How does this word deepen your understanding of what it means to reflect on God's Word?	
• What does this suggest about the quality of attention required for transformative reflection?	

3. Cross-Reference Analysis:

• Read Psalm 1:1–3. How does the psalmist describe meditation on God's law and its results?	
• Read Joshua 1:8. What connection does this verse make between meditation and action?	
• Read 2 Timothy 3:16–17. What effects does Scripture have when properly engaged with?	

4. Interpretation: What does the text mean?

• Why does James connect being "quick to listen" with receiving God's Word (v. 19)?	
• What is significant about the mirror analogy for God's Word?	
• What is the difference between being a "hearer who forgets" and a "doer who acts" (v. 25 ESV)?	
• How does James connect freedom with reflection on and obedience to God's Word?	

Theological Reflection

James reveals that true reflection on God's Word isn't passive reception but active engagement that transforms behavior. The mirror metaphor illuminates how Scripture reveals our true condition—showing us not just whom we are but whom we're meant to be in Christ. The kind of "look[ing] intently" (v. 25) James describes goes beyond casual reading to penetrating reflection that internalizes truth. This reflection directly shapes our actions, making us "doers of the word" (v. 22 ESV). Morning meditation on Scripture becomes more than a devotional exercise; it's the means by which God's truth is embedded in our hearts, guiding our responses throughout the day. By beginning the day with this kind of reflection, we position ourselves to live out what we've received rather than quickly forgetting it amid life's demands.

Personal Application

☼ **How often do you find yourself being a "hearer who forgets" rather than a "doer who acts" (v. 25 ESV)?**

- What might it look like to look "intently" (v. 25) into God's Word as part of your morning routine?

- What specific passage of Scripture has recently functioned as a "mirror" in your life, revealing something about yourself?

- What practical steps could help you connect morning reflection on Scripture with obedient action throughout the day?

PRAYER

Lord, help me to be quick to listen, slow to speak, and slow to become angry. Teach me to humbly accept Your Word planted in me, which can save me. Guard me from being merely a hearer who looks at myself in the mirror of Your Word and immediately forgets what I look like. Instead, may I look intently into Your perfect law that gives freedom, continuing in it—not forgetting what I have heard but doing it. Bless my morning reflection on Your Word, that it might bear fruit in transformed living throughout this day. In Jesus' name, amen.

DAY 5

INCORPORATING REFLECTION INTO YOUR MORNING PRACTICE

INTRODUCTION

This week, we add the practice of reflection to our growing morning routine. The Prayer of Examen helps us notice God's presence in our lives and discern His direction. This becomes the third element of your GREAT Morning Revolution, building on stillness and gratitude.

Read

> Test me, LORD, and try me, examine my heart and my mind; for I have always been mindful of your unfailing love and have lived in reliance on your faithfulness.
>
> **Psalm 26:2–3**

EXPANDING YOUR MORNING REVOLUTION

1. **Morning Stillness** (5 minutes)
   - Begin with your established practice of stillness.
   - Take several deep breaths, becoming aware of God's presence.
   - Rest in God's presence for a few minutes.
2. **Morning Gratitude** (5–7 minutes)
   - Continue your practice of thanksgiving.
   - Review specific moments of blessing from the previous day.
   - Write down 3–5 things you're grateful for in your journal.

3. Morning Reflection (10–12 minutes)

- Ask God to help you see as He sees, both your life and His presence in it.
- Review the previous day, and think about your answers to these questions:
  - When did you feel most alive, connected, or joyful?
  - When did you feel drained, disconnected, or resistant?
  - Where did you sense God's presence?
  - Where did you feel God's absence?
- Notice patterns without judgment, simply observing with curiosity.
- Invite the Holy Spirit to illuminate one or two significant moments that need attention.
- Gently examine each moment using these questions:
  - What was happening internally (thoughts, feelings, desires)?
  - How did you respond? What motivated your response?
  - Where were you aligned with God's Spirit?
  - Where did you resist or miss God's presence?
- Express gratitude for growth and, where necessary, repentance for shortcomings.

4. Looking Forward (3–5 minutes)

- Bring your attention to the day ahead.
- Ask for the grace, wisdom, and strength you need.
- Offer a prayer of commitment: "Lord, I offer this day to You. Help me to carry the insights from this reflection into each moment."
- Close by praying the Lord's Prayer out loud or silently (found on page 185).

REFLECTION QUESTIONS

What did you notice about yourself through this reflective prayer?

- How did examining yesterday in God's presence affect your approach to today?

- Was there any resistance you felt during this prayer? What might that reveal?

YOUR WEEK 3 MORNING ROUTINE

For the coming week, commit to your expanded morning practice of stillness (5 minutes), gratitude (5–7 minutes), and reflection (10–12 minutes). You might need to set your alarm 5–10 minutes earlier than last week to make space for this deepening practice.

PRAYER FOR THE WEEK AHEAD

God of wisdom and grace, thank You for the gift of reflection. As I practice looking honestly at my life in Your presence this week, guard me from both unhealthy introspection and thoughtless living. Help me to see as You see—to recognize both Your faithful presence and my need for growth. May each morning's reflection deepen my self-awareness, strengthen my attentiveness to Your Spirit, and prepare me to live more faithfully in the day ahead. Through Jesus Christ, who knows me fully and loves me completely, amen.

EXALT

LIFTING GOD'S NAME HIGH

(90 MINUTES)

WELCOME AND ICEBREAKER

(10 MINUTES)

For continuing groups, allow a few minutes for participants to reconnect.

Icebreaker: Describe a time when you felt completely in awe of God—a moment when His majesty or goodness overwhelmed you.

OPENING THEOLOGICAL REFLECTION

(5 MINUTES)

Select a volunteer to read aloud.

Worship stands at the center of human existence. We were created for it—designed to exalt something greater than ourselves. As Augustine famously observed, "Thou hast made us for thyself, O Lord, and our heart is restless until it finds its rest in thee." The question isn't *whether* we will worship but *what* we will worship.

Biblical worship—exaltation of God—is fundamentally about recognizing reality rather than creating it. When we lift God's name high, we're acknowledging whom He truly is and whom we truly are in relation to Him. This act of exaltation isn't primarily for God's benefit, as if He needed our praise to be complete. Rather, it's for our transformation. As we behold His glory, we are changed into the same image (2 Cor. 3:18).

Morning worship holds special significance in Scripture. From David's declaration "I will awaken the dawn" with praise (Ps. 57:8) to the morning sacrifices in the temple, God's people have recognized daybreak as a fitting moment to exalt the Creator of light. Beginning our day with exaltation reorients our entire lives to their proper center—not ourselves, our achievements, or our struggles, but the One who is eternally worthy of praise.

As we explore exaltation as an essential element of morning prayer, we're reclaiming our fundamental purpose as human beings—to glorify God and enjoy Him forever. This isn't about manufacturing emotional experiences but about aligning our hearts with the reality of whom God is, allowing that truth to shape everything else about our day.

OPENING PRAYER

Pray together in unison or select a volunteer:

Holy and majestic God, we come before You acknowledging that You alone are worthy of exaltation. Forgive us for the ways we have elevated other things—including ourselves—to the place that belongs only to You. As we explore worship as part of our morning prayer, open our hearts to experience You more fully. Teach us what it means to begin each day by lifting Your name high and how this practice transforms our vision of everything else. May our study lead not just to understanding but to authentic worship that glorifies You and satisfies our souls. In Jesus' name, amen.

SCRIPTURE READING BEFORE TEACHING

Read Psalm 34:1–3 and Isaiah 6:1–5 aloud.

VIDEO TEACHING

(23 MINUTES)

Watch Week 4 video "Exalt" streaming or on DVD.

NOTES

Use the space below to take notes if you'd like.

GROUP DISCUSSION

(45 MINUTES)

Leader, present each prompt, associated passages, and questions in order to the group Where scripture is to be read, select a volunteer to read aloud to the group.

1. Biblical Foundations for Morning Worship

Read Psalm 5:3 and Psalm 59:16–17, which specifically connect morning with praise.

- What significance might there be to beginning the day with praise rather than petition?
- What qualities of God do these psalms highlight as worthy of morning praise?
- How might establishing worship as your first activity shape the rest of your day?

2. Worship as Response to God's Revelation

Read Isaiah 6:1–8, where Isaiah's worship flows from his vision of God's holiness.

- What does Isaiah's response teach us about the proper reaction to God's revelation?
- How does Isaiah's awareness of his own sinfulness relate to his worship?
- What is the connection between worship and willing service in this passage?

3. Exaltation in All Circumstances

Read Habakkuk 3:17–19 and Acts 16:23–25, where worship occurs in difficult circumstances.

- What makes it possible to worship God genuinely amid suffering or lack?
- How does worship in difficult times differ from denial or spiritual bypassing?
- Share about a time when worship helped you navigate a difficult season. What made this possible?

4. The Transformative Power of Beholding

Read 2 Corinthians 3:17–18 and Psalm 115:4–8, where worship transforms worshipers.

- How does what we worship shape whom we become?
- What does it mean practically to "behold . . . the glory of the Lord" (v. 18 ESV) in morning prayer?
- How have you experienced transformation through worship?

5. Worship as Spiritual Warfare

Read 2 Chronicles 20:1–22, where worship becomes a battle strategy.

- How does beginning the day with worship prepare us for spiritual battles?
- What enemies (fear, anxiety, temptation, etc.) might morning worship help us confront?

- Why would God instruct His people to send singers ahead of the army?

6. The Content of Our Worship

Read Revelation 4:8–11 and 5:9–14, which reveal worship in heaven.

- What aspects of God's character are exalted in these passages?
- How might these heavenly worship scenes inform our morning exaltation?
- What difference would it make to begin your day conscious that you're joining in heaven's worship?

7. Practical Approaches to Morning Exaltation

- What forms might morning worship take beyond singing? (Consider Scripture reading, declaration, contemplation, etc.)
- What resources (music, prayer books, Scripture collections) might support your practice of morning exaltation?
- What practical challenges might you face in establishing worship as part of your morning routine, and how will you address them?

CLOSING REFLECTION

Ask participants to complete this sentence in writing.

MY ONE SENTENCE REQUEST

When I begin my day by exalting God, I . . .

CLOSING PRAYER

Read together or select a volunteer.

Worthy and majestic God, we join with all creation and with the hosts of heaven in lifting Your name high. You alone deserve our worship—not just on Sundays or in church gatherings, but at the start of each new day. Forgive us for how quickly we turn to our own concerns without first acknowledging Your greatness. Help us to establish the practice of morning exaltation, beginning each day by declaring Your worthiness and our devotion. As we behold Your glory in worship, transform us into Your likeness with ever-increasing glory. May the praise of our lips shape the orientation of our hearts and the actions of our hands throughout each day. In Jesus' name, amen.

LIFTING GOD'S NAME HIGH

PERSONAL BIBLE STUDY

DAY 1

THE CALL TO CONTINUAL PRAISE

Begin by stilling your heart, becoming aware of God's presence with you now.

CONTEXT SETTING

Psalm 34 begins with a remarkable commitment—to praise God continually, at all times. Written by David after he escaped a dangerous situation by feigning madness (1 Sam. 21:10–15), this psalm reveals worship not as an occasional activity but as a continuous posture of life. Today we'll explore how beginning our day with exaltation establishes a foundation for continual praise throughout the day.

Read: Psalm 34:1–10

Inductive Study

1. Observation: What does the text say?

• What commitment does David make about praise in verse 1?	
• Who does David invite to join him in worship in verses 2–3?	
• What personal testimony does David share in verses 4–7?	
• What invitation does David extend in verses 8–10?	
• What promises does David make about those who seek the Lord?	

2. Word Study: "Boast" (v. 2) The Hebrew verbal root behind "boast" is *halal*, which means "to praise or celebrate." In Psalm 34:2, David uses the form *hithallel*, a reflexive stem that conveys internal action—his soul is actively glorying in the Lord. This isn't about drawing attention to himself, but about finding joy, identity, and confidence in whom God is. It's the same root used in "Hallelujah," which means "Praise the LORD."

• How does it shape your faith to think of boasting—not in yourself—but in whom God is?	
• What might it mean for your soul to glory in the Lord as your highest source of identity?	

3. Cross-Reference Analysis:

• Read Psalm 113:3. How does this verse emphasize the continual nature of praise?	
• Read Hebrews 13:15. What does this verse call the praise we offer?	
• Read Ephesians 5:18–20. What connection does Paul make between being filled with the Spirit and continuous worship?	

4. Interpretation: What does the text mean?

• What does it mean to praise God "at all times" (v. 1)? Is this literally possible?	
• Why does David specifically invite the humble to "hear and be glad" (v. 2 ESV)?	
• What connection exists between David's testimony of deliverance and his call to worship?	
• How does the invitation to "taste and see" (v. 8) relate to the act of exalting God?	

Theological Reflection

Psalm 34 reveals praise not as a sporadic religious activity but as life's fundamental orientation. David's commitment to praise God "at all times" (v. 1) establishes worship as the continuous backdrop against which all of life unfolds. This isn't about maintaining constant emotional intensity but about a settled recognition of God's worthiness regardless of circumstances. Beginning the day with deliberate exaltation helps establish this orientation, directing our attention to God's character before the day's demands compete for our focus. Morning praise becomes the foundation for a life that continually "taste[s] and see[s]" (v. 8) God's goodness. When we start by magnifying the Lord together, we create space for our souls to "boast in the LORD" (v. 2 ESV) rather than in our own strength or accomplishments.

Personal Application

☼ **What would it mean for you to praise God "at all times" (v. 1)? How might morning exaltation help establish this rhythm?**

- David invites others to "glorify the LORD with me" and "exalt his name together" (v. 3). How might corporate aspects of worship be incorporated into your morning routine?

- David's praise flows from his testimony of God's deliverance. What personal testimonies of God's work might fuel your morning worship?

- How might beginning your day by "tast[ing] and see[ing]" (v. 8) God's goodness change your approach to challenges?

PRAYER

I will extol You, Lord, at all times; Your praise will always be on my lips. My soul will boast in You; let the humble hear and be glad. Help me to glorify Your name and exalt You together with all Your people. Thank You for answering me and delivering me from all my fears. As I look to You this morning, may my face be radiant and unashamed. Thank You for hearing my cry and saving me from all my troubles. As I begin this day, I taste and see that You are good; blessed am I as I take refuge in You. In Jesus' name, amen.

DAY 2

THE TRANSFORMING POWER OF BEHOLDING GOD'S GLORY

Begin by quieting your heart, opening yourself to behold God's glory.

CONTEXT SETTING

In 2 Corinthians 3, Paul contrasts the glory of the old covenant with the surpassing glory of the new covenant in Christ. This passage reveals a profound spiritual principle: We are transformed by what we behold. As we focus our attention on the Lord's glory, we are changed into His likeness. Today we'll explore how morning exaltation—deliberately turning our gaze toward God's glory—becomes a transformative practice that shapes whom we become.

Read: 2 Corinthians 3:7–18

Inductive Study

1. **Observation:** What does the text say?

• What contrast does Paul make between the old and new covenants?	
• What happens when someone turns to the Lord according to verse 16?	
• What connection does Paul make between the Spirit and freedom?	
• What transformation occurs as we behold the Lord's glory?	
• How does this transformation happen according to verse 18?	

2. Word Study: "Contemplate" and "Transformed" (v. 18) The Greek word for "contemplate" (*katoptrizomenoi*) means to look at something as in a mirror, to behold, or to gaze upon with careful reflection. "Transformed" (*metamorphoumetha*) means to change form, to be transformed completely, suggesting an ongoing process rather than a single event.

• How does understanding these words deepen your appreciation of what happens in worship?	
• What does this suggest about the nature and purpose of beholding God in worship?	

3. Cross-Reference Analysis:

• Read Psalm 115:4–8. What happens to those who worship idols?	
• Read Romans 12:2. How does this passage complement 2 Corinthians 3:18?	
• Read 1 John 3:2. What ultimate transformation awaits believers, and how is it connected to seeing God?	

4. Interpretation: What does the text mean?

• What is the "veil" Paul refers to, and how is it removed (vv. 13–16, 18)?	
• What does it mean practically to "contemplate the Lord's glory" (v. 18)?	
• Why does transformation come "with ever-increasing glory" (v. 18) rather than all at once?	
• What role does the Spirit play in the transformation that comes through contemplating?	

Theological Reflection

Second Corinthians 3:18 reveals a profound spiritual principle: We become like what we worship. When we turn our attention toward God's glory, we are gradually transformed into the same image. This isn't just a psychological phenomenon but a spiritual reality—the Spirit's work in conforming us to Christ's likeness as we fix our gaze on Him. Morning exaltation, then, becomes more than a devotional exercise; it's a transformative practice that shapes our character and conduct throughout the day. By beginning with deliberate focus on God's glory, we initiate a process of transformation that continues "with ever-increasing glory" (v. 18) or, in some translations, "from glory to glory" (v. 18 NKJV). Just as Moses' face reflected God's glory after being in His presence, our lives increasingly reflect Christ's character as we contemplate Him in worship.

Personal Application

☼ **What typically receives your first attention in the morning? How might deliberately turning your gaze toward God's glory first change the course of your day?**

- What veils might be hindering your ability to clearly see the LORD's glory?

- What specific aspects of God's glory could you focus on in morning worship?

- How have you experienced transformation through worship? What evidence of becoming more like Christ have you noticed?

PRAYER

Lord, I turn to You this morning, asking You to remove any veil that obscures my vision of Your glory. Thank You that where Your Spirit is, there is freedom. As I behold Your glory in worship, transform me into Your likeness with ever-increasing glory. May my first focus each day be not on myself, my tasks, or my concerns, but on the radiance of whom You are. Let my life increasingly reflect the beauty I behold in You. Shape me through the practice of morning exaltation, that I might become more like Christ today. In Jesus' name, amen.

DAY 3

EXALTATION AMID ADVERSITY

Begin by centering your heart on God's unchanging worthiness, regardless of circumstances.

CONTEXT SETTING

The book of Habakkuk records an honest dialogue between the prophet and God during a time of national calamity. Habakkuk questions God's justice as he watches Judah's sin go unpunished while the wicked Babylonians rise in power. God reveals His plan to use Babylon to judge Judah, which further confounds the prophet. Yet remarkably, the book ends not with despair but with one of Scripture's most powerful declarations of worship amid adversity. Today, we'll explore how morning exaltation becomes possible and powerful even in life's most challenging seasons.

Read: Habakkuk 3:17–19

Inductive Study

1. **Observation:** What does the text say?

• What losses or hardships does Habakkuk describe in verse 17?	
• Despite these hardships, what declaration does he make in verse 18?	
• What attributes of God does Habakkuk focus on in verse 19?	
• What imagery does he use to describe God's sustaining power?	

2. Word Study: "Rejoice" and "Joy" (v. 18) The Hebrew words for "rejoice" (*ʿālaz*) and "joy" (*gîl*) both express intense delight and exultation. They suggest not mere contentment but active, exuberant celebration—leaping for joy, being jubilant.

• How does understanding the intensity of these words deepen your appreciation of Habakkuk's declaration?	
• What does this reveal about the nature of worship amid adversity?	

3. Cross-Reference Analysis:

• Read Acts 16:23–25. How did Paul and Silas demonstrate a similar spirit in the midst of suffering?	
• Read Job 1:20–21. How does Job's response to catastrophic loss parallel Habakkuk's declaration?	
• Read Philippians 4:4. How does Paul's command to "rejoice in the Lord always" relate to Habakkuk's worship?	

4. Interpretation: What does the text mean?

• What makes Habakkuk's worship remarkable given the context?	
• What is the significance of the phrase "yet I will rejoice in the LORD" (v. 18)?	
• How does Habakkuk's focus on whom God is rather than what God does sustain his worship?	
• What does the deer/feet imagery suggest about God's sustaining grace in difficult times?	

Theological Reflection

Habakkuk 3:17–19 reveals worship not as a response to favorable circumstances but as a declaration of God's unchanging worthiness regardless of conditions. This passage doesn't minimize suffering or suggest superficial positivity; instead, it acknowledges devastating loss while still affirming God as the source of joy and strength. Habakkuk models a profound theological truth: God's worthiness of praise depends on His character, not on our prosperity. Morning exaltation amid adversity becomes a powerful act of faith—declaring God's sufficiency when everything suggests otherwise. By beginning difficult days with deliberate focus on God rather than circumstances, we establish a spiritual foundation that helps us navigate trials with perspective and hope. Like Habakkuk, we learn to rejoice not in situations but in the Lord Himself.

Personal Application

☼ **What "though" (v. 17) circumstances are you facing that challenge your worship?**

- How might beginning your day with "yet I will rejoice in the LORD" (v. 18) change your approach to current challenges?

- What attributes of God could be the focus of your morning exaltation during difficult seasons?

- How have you experienced God giving you "feet like the feet of a deer" (v. 19) in previous trials? How might remembering this fuel your worship?

PRAYER

Sovereign Lord, though I may face barrenness, lack, or loss in my life, yet I will rejoice in You. You are my strength and my shield, my ever-present help in trouble. When my resources fail, You remain my sufficiency. Make my feet like the feet of a deer, enabling me to navigate difficult terrain with grace and confidence. Help me to begin each day with exaltation, regardless of circumstances, fixing my eyes not on what is seen but on what is unseen. May my morning worship declare Your worthiness even when life is hard. I choose to rejoice in You, the God of my salvation. In Jesus' name, amen.

DAY 4

THE HOLINESS OF GOD AND OUR RESPONSE

Begin by quieting your heart, acknowledging that you stand on holy ground in God's presence.

CONTEXT SETTING

Isaiah 6 records one of Scripture's most profound worship encounters, as the prophet sees the Lord "high and lifted up" (v. 1 ESV) in the temple. This vision of God's holiness produces first undoing, then cleansing, and finally commissioning. Today, we'll explore how encountering God's holiness in morning worship shapes our self-perception, purifies our hearts, and prepares us for service throughout the day.

Read: Isaiah 6:1–8

Inductive Study

1. Observation: What does the text say?

• How is God described in verse 1?	
• What are the seraphim saying to one another in verse 3?	
• What physical effects accompany this vision according to verse 4?	
• How does Isaiah respond to the vision in verse 5?	
• What actions are taken to cleanse Isaiah in verses 6–7?	
• What question does God ask in verse 8, and how does Isaiah respond?	

2. Word Study: "Holy" (v. 3) The Hebrew word for "holy" (*qādôš*) means "set apart," "separate," "transcendent." When repeated three times as "holy, holy, holy," it forms the Hebrew superlative, emphasizing God's holiness to the highest degree.

• How does understanding this word and its repetition deepen your appreciation of what the seraphim proclaim?	
• What does this reveal about the central attribute of God being celebrated in heaven?	

3. Cross-Reference Analysis:

• Read Revelation 4:8–11. How does this heavenly worship scene echo Isaiah's vision?	
• Read Exodus 3:1–6. What similarities exist between Moses' encounter at the burning bush and Isaiah's temple vision?	
• Read 1 Peter 1:15–16. How does this passage connect God's holiness with our conduct?	

4. Interpretation: What does the text mean?

• Why does Isaiah respond with such dismay upon seeing God's holiness?	
• What is the significance of the live coal from the altar?	
• How does Isaiah's cleansing prepare him for service?	
• What connection exists between encountering God's holiness and being sent on mission?	

Theological Reflection

Isaiah 6 reveals the transformative power of encountering God's holiness through worship. This passage demonstrates a pattern that authentic worship often follows: revelation of God's nature, recognition of our sinfulness, receiving cleansing grace, and responding to God's call. The seraphim's continual cry of "holy, holy, holy" reminds us that God's holiness—His utter uniqueness and moral perfection—stands at the center of true worship. Morning exaltation that focuses on God's holiness produces similar effects in our lives: It awakens us to our need for grace, applies the cleansing work of Christ to our hearts, and prepares us for daily mission. Beginning our day by declaring "holy, holy, holy" orients us to reality—God in His transcendent majesty and we as His forgiven servants—before we face the day's demands.

Personal Application

How might contemplating God's holiness in morning worship affect your awareness of both His greatness and your need for grace?

- Isaiah's worship led to confession. What areas of your life might need confession as you come into God's holy presence?

- Isaiah's worship culminated in commissioning. How might beginning your day with exaltation prepare you for God's purposes in your daily activities?

- What spiritual practices could help you encounter God's holiness more deeply in morning worship?

PRAYER

Holy, holy, holy are You, Lord God Almighty. The whole earth is full of Your glory. As I enter Your presence in worship, I acknowledge my unworthiness before Your perfect holiness. Thank You for the cleansing blood of Jesus that purifies my lips and heart. Here I am, Lord—send me. May my morning encounter with Your holiness prepare me to represent You faithfully throughout this day. Let my words and actions reflect the transformation that comes from beholding Your glory. As the seraphim cover their faces in Your presence, I bow in reverent worship before You. In Jesus' name, amen.

DAY 5

ADDING EXALTATION TO YOUR MORNING PRACTICE

INTRODUCTION

This week, we enhance our morning routine with Lectio Divina (sacred reading), which leads naturally to exaltation—the lifting of God's name in worship. This becomes the fourth element of your GREAT Morning Revolution, building on stillness, gratitude, and reflection.

Read

I will exalt you, my God the King; I will praise your name for ever and ever. Every day I will praise you and extol your name for ever and ever. Great is the LORD and most worthy of praise; his greatness no one can fathom. One generation commends your works to another; they tell of your mighty acts. They speak of the glorious splendor of your majesty—and I will meditate on your wonderful works. They tell of the power of your awesome works—and I will proclaim your great deeds. They celebrate your abundant goodness and joyfully sing of your righteousness.

Psalm 145:1-7

EXPANDING YOUR MORNING REVOLUTION

1. **Morning Stillness** (5–7 minutes)
    - Begin with your established practice of stillness.
    - Take several deep breaths, becoming aware of God's presence.
    - Rest in God's presence briefly.

2. Morning Gratitude (10–12 minutes)

- Continue your practice of thanksgiving.
- Write down 3–5 specific things you're grateful for today.

3. Morning Reflection (5–7 minutes)

- Briefly review the previous day, noticing God's presence and your responses.
- Acknowledge both growth and areas needing grace.
- Look ahead to the day with clarity from your reflection.
- Pray the Lord's Prayer out loud or silently (found on page 185).

4. Morning Exaltation through Lectio Divina (10–15 minutes)

Lectio Divina is an ancient Christian practice of prayerful, meditative Scripture reading that invites the reader into a deeper encounter with God. Latin for "divine reading," it involves four movements: *lectio* (reading the text slowly and attentively), *meditatio* (reflecting on a word or phrase that stands out), *oratio* (responding to God in prayer), and *contemplatio* (resting in God's presence and listening). Rather than analyzing Scripture for information, Lectio Divina opens space for transformation, allowing the Holy Spirit to speak personally through the living Word.

- **Read:** Slowly read Psalm 145:1–7 or another psalm of praise, either silently or aloud.
- **Meditate:** Notice what word or phrase catches your attention. Repeat it slowly, allowing it to sink from your head into your heart.
- **Pray:** Respond to God based on the word or phrase that stood out. If it brought comfort, offer thanksgiving; if it revealed something about God's character, offer praise.
- **Contemplate:** Move beyond words into simple presence with God, resting in His love.
- **Respond in Worship:** Close with a simple expression of worship—whether a prayer, a song, or simply declaring God's goodness.

REFLECTION QUESTIONS

- What word or phrase from Scripture most resonated with you today? Why do you think this stood out?
- How did the movement from reading to meditation to prayer to contemplation deepen your worship?
- How might beginning your day with exaltation change your perspective on challenges you'll face?

YOUR WEEK 4 MORNING ROUTINE

For the coming week, commit to your expanded morning practice of stillness (3–5 minutes), gratitude (5 minutes), reflection (5–7 minutes), and exaltation (10–15 minutes). You might need to set your alarm 5–10 minutes earlier to accommodate this growing practice.

PRAYER FOR THE WEEK AHEAD

Great and majestic God, You are enthroned on the praises of Your people. As I've practiced approaching Your Word contemplatively today, help me to carry this spirit of worship into each new morning. May the words of Scripture move from my mind to my heart, kindling deeper adoration. Teach me to exalt You not just with my lips but with my life, beginning each day by declaring Your worthiness. Let my morning exaltation become the foundation that shapes my interactions, decisions, and responses throughout the day. In Jesus' name, amen.

WEEK 5

ASK

BRINGING OUR NEEDS TO GOD

GROUP TIME

(90 MINUTES)

WELCOME AND ICEBREAKER

(10 MINUTES)

For continuing groups, allow a few minutes for participants to reconnect.

Icebreaker: Share about a time when you received a surprising answer to prayer—either something you didn't expect or something that came in an unexpected way.

OPENING THEOLOGICAL REFLECTION

(5 MINUTES)

Select a volunteer to read aloud.

Prayer is a profound mystery—finite creatures communing with the infinite Creator, temporal beings engaging with the eternal God. Scripture repeatedly invites us to bring our requests to God, assuring us that He hears and responds. Yet prayer's purpose extends far beyond receiving answers to our petitions.

When Jesus taught His disciples to pray, He placed requests within a larger framework that began with God's glory ("hallowed be your name") and purposes ("your kingdom come") (Matt. 6:9–13). This reminds us that asking is not primarily about getting what we want but about aligning ourselves with what God wants. Prayer is less about changing God's mind and more about changing our hearts to beat in rhythm with His.

Morning prayer, especially, shapes our approach to the day ahead. By beginning with petition before facing challenges, we acknowledge our dependence on God rather than relying on our own strength. We invite divine wisdom to guide decisions we haven't yet made and divine grace to sustain us through difficulties we haven't yet encountered.

As Augustine beautifully expressed, "Prayer is not overcoming God's reluctance, but laying hold of His willingness." When we ask, we don't inform God of needs He doesn't know about or persuade Him to care more than He already does. Rather, we position ourselves to receive what His love already desires to give.

As we explore asking as an essential element of morning prayer, we enter into the mystery of divine-human partnership—bringing our needs to the God who knows them fully yet invites our participation in His unfolding purposes.

OPENING PRAYER

Pray together in unison or select a volunteer:

God who hears, we come before You acknowledging our deep need for Your wisdom, strength, and provision. As we explore the practice of bringing our requests to You, teach us to ask with both boldness and surrender—trusting that You hear every prayer and answer according to Your perfect wisdom. Help us to see prayer not as a mechanical transaction but as intimate communion with You. May our study deepen our understanding of what it means to ask in faith, knowing that You give good gifts to Your children. In Jesus' name, amen.

SCRIPTURE READING BEFORE TEACHING

Read Matthew 7:7–11 and Philippians 4:6–7 aloud.

VIDEO TEACHING

(28 MINUTES)

Watch Week 5 video "Ask" streaming or on DVD.

NOTES

Use the space below to take notes if you'd like.

GROUP DISCUSSION

(45 MINUTES)

Leader, present each prompt, associated passages, and questions in order to the group. Where scripture is to be read, select a volunteer to read aloud to the group.

1. The Invitation to Ask

Read Matthew 7:7–11 and James 4:2–3.

- What does Jesus' invitation to "ask," "seek," and "knock" reveal about God's character (v. 7)?
- According to these passages, what might prevent our prayers from being answered?
- How do you balance bold asking with submission to God's will?

2. Asking with Right Motives

Read James 4:2–3 and 1 John 5:14–15.

- What role do our motives play in prayer?
- How can we discern whether our requests align with God's will?
- What is the connection between knowing God's character and praying according to His will?

3. Morning Prayer as Preemptive Asking

Read Psalm 5:3 and Mark 1:35–39.

- Why might morning be a strategic time to bring requests to God?

- How does Jesus' example of early morning prayer before ministry decisions inform our own practice?

- What difference have you noticed when you bring the day's challenges to God before facing them versus praying only in the midst of difficulty?

4. Praying in Faith

Read Mark 11:22–24 and Hebrews 11:6.

- What role does faith play in bringing requests to God?

- How do you understand Jesus' teaching "believe that you have received it" (v. 24)?

- What misunderstandings about faith in prayer should we avoid?

5. Prayer as Relationship, Not Transaction

Read Luke 18:1–8 and Romans 8:26–27.

- What does the parable of the persistent widow teach us about the nature of prayer?

- How does the Spirit's intercession for us deepen our understanding of prayer beyond mere asking?

- How might viewing prayer as relationship rather than transaction change how we approach God with requests?

6. When God Seems Silent

Read 2 Corinthians 12:7–10 and Matthew 26:36–44.

- What do these passages teach us about prayers that seem to go unanswered?
- How did both Paul and Jesus respond when God answered their prayers with a no?
- How have you experienced God's grace being sufficient in times when your specific requests weren't granted?

7. From Individual to Intercessory Prayer

Read 1 Timothy 2:1–4 and Ephesians 6:18–20.

- How does intercessory prayer expand our vision beyond our own needs?
- What specific guidance do these passages give about to whom and for what to pray?
- What might change in our communities and world if Christians made morning intercession a priority?

CLOSING REFLECTION

Ask participants to complete this sentence in writing.

MY ONE SENTENCE REQUEST

When I bring my requests to God in the morning, I . . .

CLOSING PRAYER

Read together or select a volunteer.

Gracious God, we thank You for the privilege of bringing our requests before Your throne of grace. Thank You that You invite us to ask, seek, and knock, knowing that You hear every prayer and respond according to Your perfect wisdom and love. Forgive us for the times we've approached prayer as a transaction rather than relationship, or when we've prayed with selfish motives. Teach us to pray with both boldness and submission, seeking Your will above our own desires. As we practice morning prayer, help us to bring the day ahead to You—seeking Your guidance, strength, and provision before we face challenges. May our prayers become less about getting what we want and more about aligning our hearts with Yours. In Jesus' name, amen.

BRINGING OUR NEEDS TO GOD

PERSONAL BIBLE STUDY

DAY 1

THE INVITATION TO ASK

Begin by stilling your heart, acknowledging your dependence on God.

CONTEXT SETTING

In the Sermon on the Mount, Jesus gives one of Scripture's clearest invitations to bring our requests to God. Far from suggesting that prayer is presumptuous, Jesus encourages persistence and confidence, assuring His listeners that God delights to give good gifts to His children. Today we'll explore both the boldness and the trust implicit in Jesus' invitation to ask, and how morning prayer positions us to receive God's provision throughout the day.

Read: Matthew 7:7–11

Inductive Study

1. **Observation:** What does the text say?

• What three commands does Jesus give in verse 7?	
• What promise accompanies each command?	
• What everyday illustration does Jesus use in verses 9–11?	
• What comparison does Jesus make between earthly fathers and the heavenly Father?	
• What does Jesus say the Father gives to those who ask Him?	

2. **Word Study: "Ask" (v. 7)** The Greek word for "ask" (*aiteō*) is in the present imperative, suggesting continuous action: "Keep asking." It implies persistence rather than a single request. Similarly, "seek" (*zēteō*) and "knock" (*krouō*) are also present imperatives, indicating ongoing action.

• How does understanding these verbs as continuous actions deepen your appreciation of Jesus' teaching?	
• What does this suggest about the nature of prayer as a relationship rather than a transaction?	

3. **Cross-Reference Analysis:**

• Read Luke 11:5–13. How does this parallel passage expand our understanding through the parable of the friend at midnight?	
• Read James 1:5–8. What conditions does James attach to asking God for wisdom?	
• Read 1 John 5:14–15. How does this passage clarify what we can expect when we ask?	

4. Interpretation: What does the text mean?

• What does the progression from asking to seeking to knocking suggest about different levels of persistence or intensity in prayer?	
• Why does Jesus use the analogy of a father giving gifts to his children?	
• What does Jesus mean by "good gifts" (v. 11) in this passage?	
• How does this teaching balance the encouragement to ask boldly with trust in God's wisdom to give what is truly good?	

Theological Reflection

Matthew 7:7–11 reveals asking not as an optional addition to the Christian life but as a fundamental expression of our dependence on God. Jesus' encouragement to persistent asking, seeking, and knocking suggests that prayer is not merely about receiving answers but about developing relationship through continual conversation with God. The father-child analogy grounds prayer in the intimate relationship we have with God, assuring us that our requests are heard not by a reluctant deity but by a loving Father who delights to give good gifts. Morning prayer becomes a powerful expression of this dependence, acknowledging at the day's beginning that we need God's provision for whatever lies ahead. By asking before we even fully know what the day holds, we position ourselves to receive what God already desires to give.

Personal Application

- What requests have you hesitated to bring to God? How might Jesus' teaching here encourage you to pray more boldly?

- How might beginning your day by asking for God's provision change your approach to challenges that arise?

- In what ways have you experienced God giving "good gifts" (v. 11) in response to prayer, even when they weren't exactly for what you asked?

- What specific needs could you bring to God each morning this week?

PRAYER

Loving Father, thank You for Your invitation to ask, seek, and knock. I come before You acknowledging my complete dependence on Your provision. Help me to pray with both persistence and trust, confident that You hear my requests and desire to give good gifts. As I begin each day in prayer, teach me to bring my needs to You before I face challenges, trusting Your perfect wisdom to provide what is truly best. Thank You that You are not a reluctant God who must be persuaded, but a loving Father who delights to care for Your children. In Jesus' name, amen.

DAY 2

PRAYING WITH THE RIGHT HEART

Begin by quieting your heart, asking God to examine your motives.

CONTEXT SETTING

James 4 addresses conflicts within the early church, tracing their source to unmet desires and selfish ambitions. In this context, James identifies a profound problem with prayer: asking with wrong motives. This passage reveals that the effectiveness of our prayers is connected not just to our faith but to our intentions. Today we'll explore how morning prayer becomes an opportunity to align our desires with God's purposes before the day's demands pull us toward selfish ambitions.

Read: James 4:1–3

Inductive Study

1. **Observation:** What does the text say?

• What does James identify as the source of quarrels and conflicts?	
• What problem does James highlight in verse 2?	
• What reason does James give for unanswered prayer in verse 3?	
• What connection does James make between desires, prayers, and relationships?	

2. **Word Study: "Wrong motives" (v. 3)** The Greek phrase for "wrong motives" (*kakōs aiteisthe*) combines "evil" or "wrong" with "asking." The term suggests not just imperfect prayers but prayers corrupted by selfish intent, aimed at personal pleasure rather than God's purposes.

• How does understanding this phrase deepen your appreciation of what James is warning against?	
• What does this reveal about God's concern, not just with what we ask for but why we ask?	

3. Cross-Reference Analysis:

• Read Psalm 66:18. What connection does the psalmist make between heart attitude and prayer?	
• Read 1 John 3:21–22. What conditions does John connect with confidence that God hears our prayers?	
• Read Matthew 6:9–13. How does Jesus' model prayer demonstrate right motives in asking?	

4. Interpretation: What does the text mean?

• How does coveting or wrong desire corrupt not just actions but also prayers?	
• What types of requests might qualify as asking with wrong motives "that you may spend what you get on your pleasures" (v. 3)?	
• How does this passage challenge the "prosperity gospel" teaching that God wants to fulfill all our material desires?	
• What connection might exist between the conflicts described in verses 1–2 and the selfish prayers in verse 3?	

Theological Reflection

James 4:1–3 reveals a profound truth about prayer: God's response is connected not just to our faith but to our motives. This passage challenges the misconception that prayer is about getting God to fulfill our desires, showing instead that true prayer aligns our desires with God's purposes. The reference to "spend[ing] what you get on your pleasures" (v. 3) suggests that selfish prayers treat God as a means to our own ends rather than recognizing that we exist for His glory. Morning prayer becomes a critical opportunity to examine our motives before the day's activities engage our ambitions. By bringing our desires to God at the day's beginning, we invite Him to purify our motives and align our requests with His kingdom purposes rather than our personal pleasure.

Personal Application

- What desires tend to dominate your prayer life? Take time to honestly examine whether these reflect God's priorities or your own pleasures.

- How might beginning your day by surrendering your desires to God help purify your motives throughout the day?

- What specific area of your life needs realignment from selfish ambition to kingdom purpose?

- How could your morning prayers reflect a greater concern for God's glory than your own comfort or success?

PRAYER

Searching God, You know the depths of my heart better than I know myself. Examine my motives as I come before You in prayer. Forgive me for the times I have treated prayer as a means to my own ends, seeking Your gifts rather than Your presence. As I begin each day in prayer, purify my desires and align my heart with Your kingdom purposes. Teach me to ask not merely for what pleases me but for what glorifies You. Transform my prayers from selfish petitions to kingdom-advancing requests. In Jesus' name, amen.

DAY 3

CASTING ALL ANXIETIES ON HIM

Begin by taking a deep breath, releasing your anxieties into God's care.

CONTEXT SETTING

In a letter written to persecuted Christians facing severe trials, Peter offers profound guidance for dealing with anxiety. Rather than suggesting stoic endurance or simplistic positive thinking, he invites believers to bring their anxieties to God in prayer. Today we'll explore how morning prayer becomes a powerful practice for releasing our concerns to God before they consume our thoughts throughout the day.

Read: 1 Peter 5:5–11

Inductive Study

1. Observation: What does the text say?

• What instruction does Peter give regarding anxiety in verse 7?	
• What virtue does Peter emphasize in verses 5–6?	
• What reason does Peter give for casting our anxieties on God?	
• What warning does Peter give in verse 8?	
• What promise does Peter make in verse 10?	

2. Word Study: "Cast" and "Anxieties" (v. 7) The Greek word for "cast" (*epiripsantes*) means "to throw upon" or "place upon," suggesting complete transfer of a burden. "Anxiety" (*merimnan*) refers to distracting concerns that divide the mind and disrupt inner peace.

• How does understanding these words deepen your appreciation of what Peter is instructing?	
• What does the imagery of "cast[ing]" (v. 7) or throwing suggest about how completely God wants us to transfer our concerns to Him?	

3. Cross-Reference Analysis:

• Read Psalm 55:22. How does this verse parallel Peter's instruction?	
• Read Philippians 4:6–7. What additional guidance does Paul give about handling anxiety?	
• Read Matthew 6:25–34. How do Jesus' teachings on worry (the verb form of the same Greek noun Peter and Paul are using) complement Peter's instruction?	

4. Interpretation: What does the text mean?

• Why does Peter connect humility (vv. 5–6) with casting anxieties on God (v. 7)?	
• What does the phrase "because he cares for you" (v. 7) reveal about the basis for trusting God with our concerns?	
• How does awareness of spiritual opposition (v. 8) relate to the practice of casting anxieties on God?	
• What connection exists between enduring suffering (v. 9) and God's promise to restore and strengthen (v. 10)?	

Theological Reflection

The invitation to cast our anxieties on God in 1 Peter 5:7 is grounded in the profound truth that "he cares for you"—a revolutionary concept in a world where gods were typically viewed as distant and indifferent. Peter places this instruction in the context of humility, suggesting that holding onto our anxieties often stems from pride—the illusion that we can control outcomes through worry. Morning prayer becomes a powerful application of this teaching, allowing us to transfer our concerns to God at the day's beginning rather than carrying them ourselves. By casting our anxieties on God before facing the day's challenges, we position ourselves to resist the enemy (v. 9) from a place of peace rather than fear.

Personal Application

- What specific anxieties are you carrying right now that you need to cast on God?

- How might beginning your day by deliberately transferring your concerns to God change your experience of anxiety?

- In what ways might pride be preventing you from fully casting your anxieties on God?

- What practical method could help you visualize or experience the act of "cast[ing]" your cares on God during morning prayer (v. 7)?

PRAYER

Caring Father, I humble myself under Your mighty hand, knowing that You will lift me up in due time. This morning, I cast all my anxiety on You, acknowledging that You care deeply for me. Free me from the pride that makes me think I must carry my burdens alone. Help me to resist the enemy, standing firm in faith, confident that You will restore, establish, strengthen, and support me. As I begin this day, I transfer my concerns from my shoulders to Yours, trusting in Your perfect love and care. May this practice of morning release guard my heart and mind throughout the day. In Jesus' name, amen.

DAY 4

PRAYER IN THE FACE OF IMPOSSIBILITY

Begin by acknowledging God's limitless power, surrendering your perception of what's possible.

CONTEXT SETTING

Mark 11 records Jesus' dramatic action of cursing a fig tree and cleansing the temple, displaying His authority over religious systems that bore no fruit. In this context, Jesus offers profound teaching about prayer and faith, challenging His disciples to believe that nothing is impossible with God. Today we'll explore how morning prayer becomes an encounter with divine possibility before we face seemingly insurmountable challenges throughout the day.

Read: Mark 11:20–25

Inductive Study

1. Observation: What does the text say?

• What did Peter notice about the fig tree in verse 20?	
• What instruction does Jesus give about faith in verse 22?	
• What specific example of seemingly impossible prayer does Jesus give in verse 23?	
• What promise does Jesus make about prayer in verse 24?	
• What condition does Jesus attach to prayer in verse 25?	

2. Word Study: "Believe" (v. 24) The Greek word for "believe" (*pisteuete*) is in the present tense, suggesting ongoing faith rather than a momentary act of believing. The phrase "have received" (*elabete*) is in the aorist tense, suggesting completed action, though the fulfillment may still be future.

• How does understanding these tenses deepen your appreciation of what Jesus is teaching?	
• What does this suggest about the nature of faith as it relates to prayer?	

3. Cross-Reference Analysis:

• Read Hebrews 11:1. How does this definition of faith relate to Jesus' teaching about believing "that you have received" (v. 24)?	
• Read James 1:5–8. What does James say about doubting when asking God for something?	
• Read 2 Corinthians 5:7. How does Paul's teaching about walking by faith connect with Jesus' instruction in Mark 11?	

4. Interpretation: What does the text mean?

• What is the significance of Jesus telling His disciples to "have faith in God" (v. 22) rather than simply "have faith"?	
• What does the mountain-moving imagery teach us about bringing seemingly impossible situations to God?	
• How should we understand Jesus' statement about believing "that you have received it" (v. 24) when the fulfillment isn't yet visible?	
• Why does Jesus connect forgiveness with effective prayer?	

Theological Reflection

Mark 11:22–25 reveals prayer not as wishful thinking but as confident engagement with God's unlimited power. Jesus' instruction to "have faith in God" (v. 22) grounds prayer not in positive thinking or self-confidence but in the character and ability of God Himself. The mountain-moving imagery graphically illustrates that prayer confronts impossibility with divine possibility. The call to believe we "have received" (v. 24) what we ask for challenges our linear understanding of time, inviting us to live in the tension of "already but not yet"—treating God's promises as accomplished even before visible fulfillment. Morning prayer becomes a powerful arena for this kind of faith, allowing us to bring seemingly insurmountable challenges to God at the day's beginning and to walk forward in confidence that He is already at work. By beginning with impossibility-confronting prayer, we approach the day through the lens of God's power rather than our limitations.

Personal Application

What "mountains" in your life need to be brought to God in faith-filled prayer?

How might beginning your day by declaring God's power over impossibilities change your approach to challenges?

- In what ways have you struggled with believing you "have received" (v. 24) what you've asked for before seeing visible evidence?

- What relationships might need forgiveness as part of your morning prayer practice?

PRAYER

Almighty God, I have faith in You—in Your character, Your power, and Your willingness to act on behalf of Your children. This morning, I bring before You the mountains that stand in my way, declaring that nothing is impossible for You. I believe that You not only can but will move in these situations according to Your perfect will. I choose to believe that I have received what I ask for, walking by faith and not by sight. Search my heart for any unforgiveness, and help me to forgive as I have been forgiven. May my morning prayers be characterized by mountain-moving faith rather than doubt. In Jesus' name, amen.

DAY 5

INCORPORATING ASKING INTO YOUR MORNING PRACTICE

INTRODUCTION

This week, we expand our morning practice with intercessory prayer—bringing not only our needs but also the needs of others before God's throne. This becomes the fifth element of your GREAT Morning Revolution, building on stillness, gratitude, reflection, and exaltation.

Read

I urge, then, first of all, that petitions, prayers, intercession and thanksgiving be made for all people—for kings and all those in authority, that we may live peaceful and quiet lives in all godliness and holiness. This is good, and pleases God our Savior, who wants all people to be saved and to come to a knowledge of the truth. For there is one God and one mediator between God and mankind, the man Christ Jesus, who gave himself as a ransom for all people. This has now been witnessed to at the proper time.

1 Timothy 2:1–6

EXPANDING YOUR MORNING REVOLUTION

1. Morning Stillness (3 minutes)

- Begin with your established practice of stillness.
- Take several deep breaths, becoming aware of God's presence.

2. Morning Gratitude (3–5 minutes)

- Continue your practice of thanksgiving.
- Briefly note three things you're grateful for today.

3. Morning Reflection (5 minutes)

- Briefly review the previous day, noticing God's presence and your responses.
- Acknowledge both growth and areas needing grace.

4. Morning Exaltation (5–7 minutes)

- Read a psalm or scripture passage that exalts God.
- Respond in worship through prayer, song, or declaration of God's attributes.
- Pray the Lord's Prayer out loud or silently (found on page 185).

5. Morning Asking Through Intercessory Prayer (15–20 minutes)

- Move outward in your intercession like expanding ripples in a pond.
- **Circle 1: Those Closest to You** (3–4 minutes)
    - Bring family members and close friends before God.
    - Pray for their specific needs and spiritual growth.
- **Circle 2: Your Community** (3–4 minutes)
    - Pray for neighbors, coworkers, church members, and local connections.
    - Consider specific needs facing your community.
- **Circle 3: Those in Authority** (3–4 minutes)
    - Following Paul's instruction, pray for government leaders at all levels.
    - Include prayers for teachers, employers, church leaders, and others in authority.
- **Circle 4: The Suffering** (3–4 minutes)
    - Bring before God those experiencing poverty, persecution, illness, or injustice.
    - Include both people you know personally and global situations.

- **Circle 5: Global Concerns** (3–4 minutes)
  - Pray for nations, peoples, and situations around the world.
  - Include prayers for the advance of the gospel among unreached peoples.

6. Surrendering the Results (2–3 minutes)

- Acknowledge that God sees the full picture beyond what you can see.
- Surrender your expectations about how and when God will answer.
- Thank God for His faithfulness to hear and respond according to His perfect wisdom.

REFLECTION QUESTIONS

- How did praying for others at the beginning of your day shift your perspective?

- Was there a particular person or situation that seemed especially impressed on your heart during this prayer time?

- How might regular morning intercession change your approach to relationships and global concerns?

YOUR WEEK 5 MORNING ROUTINE

For the coming week, commit to your expanded morning practice of stillness (3 minutes), gratitude (3–5 minutes), reflection (5 minutes), exaltation (5–7 minutes), and asking through intercessory prayer (15–20 minutes). You might need to set your alarm 10–15 minutes earlier to accommodate this growing practice.

PRAYER FOR THE WEEK AHEAD

Sovereign God, thank You for the privilege of intercessory prayer—for the opportunity to participate in Your redemptive work through bringing others before Your throne of grace. As I move through this week, help me to begin each day by looking beyond my own needs to the concerns of others. Teach me to pray with both faith and surrender, trusting that You hear every prayer and answer according to Your perfect wisdom. May my morning intercession align my heart with Your kingdom purposes and prepare me to be Your instrument of blessing throughout the day. In Jesus' name, amen.

TRUST

SURRENDERING OUR DAY TO GOD

(90 MINUTES)

WELCOME AND ICEBREAKER

(10 MINUTES)

For continuing groups, allow a few minutes for participants to reconnect.

Icebreaker: Describe a situation where you had to trust God with an outcome you couldn't control. What made it difficult to trust, and what helped you surrender the situation to Him?

OPENING THEOLOGICAL REFLECTION

(5 MINUTES)

Select a volunteer to read aloud.

Trust stands at the very heart of our relationship with God. From Genesis to Revelation, Scripture portrays faith not as intellectual assent to doctrines but as radical trust in a Person—confidence in God's character even when His ways remain mysterious. The Hebrew word most often translated as "trust" (*bātakh*) may possibly carry the sense of lying helpless face down—a posture of complete vulnerability and dependence.

This kind of trust runs counter to our culture's emphasis on self-reliance and control. We're taught from childhood to take charge of our lives, to have backup plans, to never fully depend on anyone else. Yet the gospel calls us to a different way—surrendering outcomes to the One whose wisdom and love far exceed our own.

Morning provides a unique opportunity for this sacred surrender. By beginning our day with deliberate trust, we acknowledge that the hours ahead are not ultimately under our control. We release our grip on outcomes before facing situations that tempt us to worry or become self-reliant. This isn't passive resignation but active faith—choosing to place our day in the hands of the One who holds all things together.

This threefold trust becomes a foundation for approaching life not with anxiety but with confident hope in the God who is trustworthy in all His ways.

As we explore trust as the culmination of our GREAT morning practice, we engage with both the challenge and comfort of surrender—relinquishing control while resting in the everlasting arms of a faithful God.

OPENING PRAYER

Pray together in unison or select a volunteer:

Faithful God, we come before You acknowledging our struggle to truly trust. We confess that we often prefer control to surrender, certainty to faith. As we explore what it means to begin each day by trusting You, soften our hearts to receive this truth: that in releasing our grip, we find freedom; in surrendering our plans, we discover Your perfect purposes. Teach us to trust not just with our words but with our lives, beginning each new day with open hands rather than clenched fists. In Jesus' name, amen.

SCRIPTURE READING BEFORE TEACHING

Read Proverbs 3:5–6 and Isaiah 26:3–4 aloud.

VIDEO TEACHING

(20 MINUTES)

Watch Week 6 video "Trust" streaming or on DVD.

NOTES

Use the space below to take notes if you'd like.

GROUP DISCUSSION

(45 MINUTES)

Leader, present each prompt, associated passages, and questions in order to the group. Where scripture is to be read, select a volunteer to read aloud to the group.

1. Biblical Foundations of Trust

Read Proverbs 3:5–6 and Psalm 37:3–7a.

- What specific instructions about trust do these passages give?

- What does it mean to trust with "all your heart" (3:5) rather than leaning on your own understanding?

- How does trust relate to the other disciplines we've studied (gratitude, reflection, exaltation, asking)?

2. Trust in God's Character

Read Psalm 9:10 and Isaiah 26:3–4.

- How does knowing God's character (His "name") foster trust?

- What specific attributes of God do you find most helpful when struggling to trust?

- How might beginning your day by focusing on God's trustworthy character change your approach to challenges?

3. Surrender versus Control

Read Matthew 6:25–34 and Luke 12:22–31.

- What reasons does Jesus give for not worrying?
- How does worry reveal our struggle to trust?
- What practical steps can help us move from anxiety to surrender?

4. Morning Trust as Preparation

Read Psalm 5:3 and Lamentations 3:22–23.

- Why might morning be a strategic time to practice trust?
- How does trust in the morning prepare us for challenges later in the day?
- What morning practices have helped you cultivate trust?

5. Trust in Seasons of Trial

Read Job 13:15, Habakkuk 3:17–19, and 2 Corinthians 1:8–10.

- What makes trust particularly challenging during suffering?
- How did these biblical figures maintain trust amid severe trials?
- Share about a time when trusting God during difficulty deepened your faith.

6. From Trust to Obedience

Read Genesis 22:1–18, John 14:15, and James 2:14–26.

- What connection exists between trust and obedience?
- How does Abraham's story illustrate this connection?
- How might morning surrender to God's will prepare us for faithful action throughout the day?

7. Trust as a Communal Practice

Read 2 Corinthians 1:3–11 and Hebrews 10:24–25.

- How does the community of faith help us trust God when our individual faith falters?
- What role does shared testimony play in strengthening trust?
- How might we support one another in the daily practice of trust?

CLOSING REFLECTION

Ask participants to complete this sentence in writing.

MY ONE SENTENCE REQUEST

I want to begin my days with trust because . . .

CLOSING PRAYER

Read together or select a volunteer.

Trustworthy God, we come to You with open hands, surrendering our desire for control and certainty. Thank You for Your unchanging character that makes You worthy of our deepest trust. Help us to begin each day by deliberately placing our plans, concerns, and desires in Your capable hands. When anxious thoughts arise, remind us of Your faithful presence. When challenges tempt us to rely on our own understanding, guide us back to trust in Your perfect wisdom. May our mornings become sacred moments of surrender, preparing us to walk through each day with confident trust in Your unfailing love. In Jesus' name, amen.

SURRENDERING OUR DAY TO GOD

PERSONAL BIBLE STUDY

DAY 1

THE HEART OF TRUST

Begin by releasing your grip on concerns, opening your hands in surrender to God.

CONTEXT SETTING

Proverbs 3:5–6 offers one of Scripture's clearest and most beloved instructions about trust. Written by Solomon to guide his son in wisdom, these verses appear deceptively simple yet contain profound insight about the nature of true trust. Today we'll explore what it means to trust God with our whole heart, examining both the challenge and the promise embedded in this timeless counsel.

Read: Proverbs 3:5–7

Inductive Study

1. Observation: What does the text say?

• What command is given in verse 5a?	
• What warning follows in verse 5b?	
• What areas of life should be submitted to God according to verse 6a?	
• What promise accompanies these instructions in verse 6b?	
• What additional warning is given in verse 7?	

2. Word Study: "Trust" and "Lean" (v. 5) The Hebrew word for "trust" (*batach*) carries the sense of feeling safe or secure, having confidence in someone. It suggests reliance on another rather than oneself. "Lean" (*sha'an*) means "to support oneself against something, to rely on it for stability."

• How do these word meanings deepen your understanding of what Solomon is instructing?	
• What does the imagery of "lean[ing]" (v. 5) suggest about our natural tendency toward self-reliance?	

3. Cross-Reference Analysis:

• Read Psalm 62:8. What additional insight does this verse provide about whole-hearted trust?	
• Read Jeremiah 9:23–24. How does this passage relate to the warning against leaning on our own understanding?	
• Read Isaiah 55:8–9. How does this passage help explain why trusting God rather than our understanding is wise?	

4. Interpretation: What does the text mean?

• What does it mean to trust God with "all your heart" (v. 5) versus partial trust?	
• Why is leaning on our own understanding contrasted with trusting God?	
• What does it mean practically to "acknowledge him" "in all your ways" (v. 6 ESV)?	
• What kind of "paths" (v. 6) might God make straight as we trust Him?	

Theological Reflection

Proverbs 3:5–6 reveals trust not as a compartmentalized religious activity but as a comprehensive life orientation. The command to trust with "all your heart" (v. 5) challenges our tendency toward divided allegiance—partly trusting God while hedging our bets with backup plans rooted in human wisdom. The warning against leaning on our understanding acknowledges the limits of human perception and wisdom compared to God's omniscience. Morning trust becomes a strategic practice precisely because it establishes this orientation before the day's activities tempt us toward self-reliance. By deliberately acknowledging God "in all [our] ways" (v. 6) at the day's beginning, we establish a foundation for recognizing His presence and guidance in every situation we encounter. The promise of straight paths doesn't guarantee absence of difficulty but assures us of divine guidance when we surrender control.

Personal Application

- **In what areas of your life do you find it most difficult to trust God with "all your heart" (v. 5)?**

- **How might beginning your day by deliberately choosing trust rather than self-reliance change your approach to decisions and challenges?**

- What specific ways could you acknowledge God "in all your ways" (v. 6) as part of your morning routine?

- Where do you need God to "make your paths straight" (v. 6) in your current season of life?

PRAYER

Lord, I trust in You with all my heart, choosing not to lean on my own understanding. Help me to acknowledge You in all my ways, remembering that You alone can make my paths straight. Forgive my tendency toward self-reliance and divided trust. As I begin this day, I surrender my plans, concerns, and desires to Your perfect wisdom. Guide me in decisions both large and small, that my life may reflect complete trust in Your goodness and sovereignty. In Jesus' name, amen.

DAY 2

PERFECT PEACE THROUGH TRUST

Begin by quieting your mind, allowing your scattered thoughts to settle into God's presence.

CONTEXT SETTING

Isaiah 26 forms part of a song of praise within Isaiah's "Apocalypse" (chapters 24–27), which describes God's final judgment and salvation. Amid vivid imagery of destruction and restoration, verses 3–4 offer a profound promise of peace through trust. Written during a turbulent period in Israel's history, these verses speak directly to our anxious hearts today. We'll explore how morning trust establishes a foundation of peace that sustains us through life's inevitable challenges.

Read: Isaiah 26:1–4

Inductive Study

1. Observation: What does the text say?

• What does Isaiah say God will do according to verse 1?	
• Who will enter the gates according to verse 2?	
• What promise is given in verse 3?	
• What condition is attached to this promise?	
• What reason is given for trust in verse 4?	

2. **Word Study: "Perfect Peace" (v. 3)** The Hebrew phrase for "perfect peace" is *shalom shalom*—a repetition that creates emphasis, suggesting complete or perfect peace. *Shalom* means more than absence of conflict; it implies wholeness, harmony, and well-being in every dimension of life.

• How does understanding this phrase deepen your appreciation of what God promises?	
• What does this suggest about the quality of peace available through trust?	

3. **Cross-Reference Analysis:**

• Read Philippians 4:6–7. How does this New Testament passage complement Isaiah's teaching about peace through trust?	
• Read John 14:27. How does Jesus' promise of peace relate to the peace described in Isaiah 26:3?	
• Read Romans 8:6. What connection does Paul make between the mind and peace?	

4. Interpretation: What does the text mean?

• What does it mean to have a "steadfast" mind (v. 3) in this context?	
• Why is trust the pathway to perfect peace?	
• What is the significance of God being an "everlasting rock" (v. 4 ESV) in relation to trust?	
• How does the broader context of God's protection (vv. 1–2) relate to the promise of peace?	

Theological Reflection

Isaiah 26:1–4 reveals peace not as the absence of external conflict but as an internal state anchored in trust. The promise of "perfect peace" (*shalom shalom*) (v. 3) offers not mere tranquility but comprehensive well-being that remains stable even when circumstances are not. The condition—a mind stayed or fixed on God—suggests that peace flows from focused trust rather than divided attention. Morning trust becomes a powerful practice precisely because it helps establish this mental fixation on God before the distractions and anxieties of the day compete for our focus. By deliberately anchoring our minds on the everlasting Rock at the day's beginning, we create a foundation of peace that can sustain us through whatever challenges arise. This isn't about manufacturing positive feelings but about aligning ourselves with the unchanging reality of God's faithfulness.

Personal Application

☼ **What anxieties or concerns currently disrupt your experience of God's perfect peace?**

- How might beginning your day by fixing your mind on God rather than problems change your experience of peace?

- What specific attributes of God as the "Rock eternal" (v. 4) could you focus on during morning prayer?

- What practical methods could help you maintain a mind "stayed on [God]" (v. 3 ESV) throughout the day?

PRAYER

Rock Eternal, I fix my mind on You as I begin this day. Thank You for Your promise of perfect peace—not just absence of conflict but wholeness in every dimension. Keep my mind steadfast in trust, not wavering between faith and fear. When anxious thoughts arise, help me return to this anchor: that You are trustworthy in all Your ways. May the peace established in morning trust sustain me through whatever challenges this day brings. In You alone, Lord, I place my eternal confidence. In Jesus' name, amen.

DAY 3
TRUST IN TIMES OF TESTING

Begin by acknowledging God's faithfulness in past trials, creating a foundation for present trust.

CONTEXT SETTING

Habakkuk prophesied during Judah's final years before the Babylonian invasion—a time of internal corruption and impending judgment. His book records an honest dialogue with God as he struggles to reconcile divine justice with apparent evil. After questioning God's methods, Habakkuk concludes with one of Scripture's most powerful declarations of trust amid desolation. Today we'll explore how morning trust prepares us not just for prosperity but for times of loss and testing.

Read: Habakkuk 3:16–19

Inductive Study

1. Observation: What does the text say?

• What physical and emotional response does Habakkuk describe in verse 16?	
• What devastating conditions does he anticipate in verse 17?	
• Despite these conditions, what declaration does he make in verse 18?	
• What imagery does he use to describe God's sustaining strength?	

2. Word Study: "Yet" (v. 18) The Hebrew conjunction translated "yet" (*waw*) creates a contrast between the devastating conditions described in verse 17 and Habakkuk's response of joy. It emphasizes the deliberate choice to rejoice despite circumstances.

• How does understanding this word deepen your appreciation of Habakkuk's declaration?	
• What does this reveal about the nature of trust during hardship?	

3. Cross-Reference Analysis:

• Read Job 13:15. How does Job's declaration parallel Habakkuk's trust?	
• Read 2 Corinthians 4:8–10. How does Paul's testimony complement Habakkuk's perspective?	
• Read James 1:2–4. What connection does James make between trials and spiritual maturity?	

4. Interpretation: What does the text mean?

• What makes Habakkuk's declaration of trust so remarkable given the context?	
• Why does Habakkuk focus specifically on God as "the God of my salvation" (v. 18 ESV)?	
• What is the significance of the deer/heights imagery in verse 19?	
• How does Habakkuk's experience show the relationship between honest questioning and mature faith?	

Theological Reflection

Habakkuk 3:16–19 reveals trust not as denial of difficulty but as deliberate choice amid desolation. Habakkuk doesn't minimize the severity of coming judgment or pretend it won't be painful—he acknowledges both his fear (v. 16) and the devastating losses ahead (v. 17). Yet his trust transcends circumstances, allowing him to rejoice not in conditions but in God Himself. Morning trust becomes particularly powerful during seasons of hardship precisely because it establishes this transcendent perspective before the day's challenges threaten to overwhelm us. By beginning with "yet I will rejoice in the LORD" (v. 18) rather than fixating on losses, we create a foundation of joy that difficulties cannot easily shake. Habakkuk's testimony reminds us that mature faith doesn't require prosperity—it flourishes even in devastation when anchored in God's unchanging character.

Personal Application

What "though" (v. 17) circumstances are you currently facing that challenge your trust?

- How might beginning your day with "yet I will rejoice in the LORD" (v. 18) change your experience of these challenges?

- What specific aspects of "the God of my salvation" (v. 18 ESV) could you focus on during morning prayer?

- In what areas do you need God to give you "feet like the feet of a deer" (v. 19) to navigate difficult terrain?

PRAYER

Sovereign Lord, though I may face loss, lack, or devastation, yet I will rejoice in You. You are the God of my salvation, my strength in weakness, my hope in despair. When my resources fail, You remain my sufficiency. Make my feet like the feet of the deer, enabling me to navigate difficult terrain with grace and confidence. Help me to begin each day with trust that transcends circumstances, fixing my eyes not on what is seen but on Your unchanging character. I choose to rejoice in You, regardless of conditions, for You are worthy of trust even in the darkest valley. In Jesus' name, amen.

DAY 4

FROM ANXIETY TO TRUST

Begin by releasing your anxious thoughts to God, allowing His peace to fill the space they occupied.

CONTEXT SETTING

In the Sermon on the Mount, Jesus addresses one of humanity's most persistent struggles: anxiety about basic needs and future provision. Speaking to people living with economic uncertainty and political oppression, Jesus doesn't dismiss their legitimate concerns but redirects their focus from worry to trust. Today we'll explore how morning trust offers an alternative to anxiety, establishing a foundation of confidence in God's care before the day's demands trigger worry.

Read: Matthew 6:25–34

Inductive Study

1. **Observation:** What does the text say?

• What command does Jesus repeat throughout this passage?	
• What examples from nature does Jesus use to illustrate God's care?	
• What question does Jesus ask about the value of worry in verse 27?	
• What does Jesus identify as the root of anxiety in verse 30?	
• What alternative does Jesus offer to worry in verses 33–34?	

2. **Word Study: "Worry" and "Anxious" (v. 25)** The Greek word often translated as "to worry" (*merimnaō*) refers to being anxious or troubled with cares. While some have noted its root parts could suggest the idea of being "divided" or "distracted," scholars caution against relying too heavily on etymology alone to define a word's meaning. In Scripture, *merimnaō* consistently conveys a sense of mental strain—being pulled away from trust and peace by life's burdens.

• How does this understanding help you recognize the nature of anxiety as something that pulls your focus away from God's presence?	
• How might morning prayer re-center you in God's peace rather than the fragmentation of worry?	

3. **Cross-Reference Analysis:**

• Read Philippians 4:6–7. What alternative to anxiety does Paul offer?	
• Read 1 Peter 5:6–7. What connection does Peter make between humility and casting anxieties on God?	
• Read Luke 12:22–34. How does this parallel passage expand Jesus' teaching?	

4. Interpretation: What does the text mean?

• Why does Jesus use examples from nature to address worry?	
• What does Jesus mean by identifying worriers as "you of little faith" (v. 30)?	
• How does seeking God's kingdom first relate to freedom from anxiety?	
• What practical wisdom is contained in the instruction to focus on today rather than tomorrow?	

Theological Reflection

Matthew 6:25–34 reveals worry as misplaced focus stemming from "little faith" (v. 30). Jesus doesn't trivialize genuine concerns about provision but redirects attention from self-sufficiency to divine care. His examples from nature demonstrate not just God's ability but His willingness to provide—if He cares for birds and flowers, how much more does He care for His children? Morning trust becomes a powerful antidote to anxiety precisely because it establishes proper focus before the day's concerns compete for our attention. By beginning with deliberate trust in God's care, we create a foundation that helps us navigate legitimate needs without fragmenting our minds through worry. Seeking first God's kingdom—making His priorities our focus—doesn't eliminate responsibility but places it within the larger context of divine provision.

Personal Application

- **What specific concerns tend to trigger worry in your life?**

- How might beginning your day focused on God's care rather than potential problems reduce worry?

- What evidences of God's provision—like Jesus' examples from nature—could remind you of His faithfulness?

- What would it look like to seek first God's kingdom in the midst of your current responsibilities and concerns?

PRAYER

Heavenly Father, I release my worried thoughts about provision, security, and tomorrow's needs. Thank You for caring more deeply for me than for the birds You feed and the flowers You clothe. Forgive my "little faith" that leads to divided focus and worry. As I begin this day, help me to seek first Your kingdom and righteousness, trusting that all these things will be added as well. Give me grace to focus on today's challenges without borrowing tomorrow's troubles. Replace my anxiety with confident trust in Your perfect care. In Jesus' name, amen.

DAY 5

COMPLETING YOUR GREAT MORNING ROUTINE WITH TRUST

INTRODUCTION

This week, we complete our morning revolution with centering prayer—a practice that embodies surrender and trust. With this final element, you now have established a complete GREAT Morning Revolution: Gratitude, Reflection, Exaltation, Asking, and Trusting. This framework will transform not just your mornings but your entire approach to each day.

Read

> "Be still, and know that I am God; I will be exalted among the nations, I will be exalted in the earth." The LORD Almighty is with us; the God of Jacob is our fortress.
>
> **Psalm 46:10–11**

YOUR COMPLETE GREAT MORNING REVOLUTION

1. **Morning Stillness** (2–3 minutes)
   - Begin with several deep breaths, centering yourself in God's presence.
   - Take a moment to recognize that God is already present, waiting for you.
2. **Gratitude** (5 minutes)
   - Express thanksgiving for 3–5 specific blessings.
   - Notice both obvious gifts and subtle graces from the previous day.
   - Record these in your journal.

3. Reflect (5–7 minutes)

- Review the previous day in God's presence.
- Notice moments of connection and disconnection.
- Acknowledge growth and areas needing grace.
- Look ahead to the day with insights from your reflection.

4. Exalt (5–7 minutes)

- Read a psalm or other Scripture passage that exalts God.
- Respond in worship through prayer, song, or declaration of God's attributes.
- Allow God's Word to kindle adoration in your heart.
- Pray the Lord's Prayer out loud or silently (found on page 185).

5. Ask (5–10 minutes)

- Bring your personal needs before God.
- Intercede for others in expanding circles of concern.
- Pray with both boldness and surrender to God's wisdom.

6. Trust Through Centering Prayer (10–15 minutes)

- Choose a sacred word that symbolizes your intention to consent to God's presence and action (e.g., Jesus, Peace, Trust, Love).
- Sit in silence, gently introducing your sacred word.
- When thoughts arise, don't resist them but gently return to your sacred word.
- Rest in God's presence, allowing Him to work within you beyond words or thoughts.
- Close by slowly transitioning back to awareness of your surroundings.
- Remember that this practice embodies the trust that is the culmination of your morning routine—releasing control, agendas, and outcomes to God.

REFLECTION ON YOUR GREAT MORNING REVOLUTION

- How has establishing this morning routine transformed your relationship with God?

- Which element of the GREAT practice (Gratitude, Reflect, Exalt, Ask, Trust) has been most meaningful to you, and why?

- What challenges have you overcome in establishing this routine?

- How has beginning your day with God changed your approach to daily challenges and opportunities?

SUSTAINING YOUR MORNING REVOLUTION

Now that you've established your complete GREAT Morning routine, here are some tips for sustaining it:

1. **Be flexible but consistent.** Some days may require a shorter practice, while others allow for more extended time. The key is showing up day after day.
2. **Adapt to seasons.** Your routine may look different during busy seasons, travel, or illness. Create a "minimum viable practice" for challenging times.
3. **Find accountability.** Consider sharing your morning commitment with a friend who can check in regularly.
4. **Notice the fruit.** Pay attention to how this practice is changing you over time. Record insights and transformations in your journal.
5. **Extend grace to yourself.** Remember that this is about relationship, not performance. When you miss a morning, simply begin again the next day.

PRAYER FOR THE JOURNEY AHEAD

Faithful God, thank You for the gift of mornings—for the opportunity to begin each day in Your presence before facing the world's demands. As I continue this GREAT Morning Revolution, help me to show up consistently, bringing my whole self to our time together. May the practices of Gratitude, Reflection, Exaltation, Asking, and Trusting become deeply embedded in my life, transforming not just my mornings but my entire approach to life. Thank You for meeting me in the stillness of dawn, day after day. May my morning revolution continue to bear fruit in every area of my life. In Jesus' name, amen.

CONCLUSION

Developing Your Personal Morning Revolution

As we conclude our journey through the GREAT Morning Revolution, take a moment to reflect on how far you've come. Over these six weeks, you've explored profound spiritual practices that have the potential to transform not just your mornings but your entire life.

You've discovered that morning prayer isn't about perfection but presence—showing up to meet with God before meeting the demands of the day. You've learned that even those who don't consider themselves "morning people" can develop habits that welcome God's presence at the dawn of each new day.

The GREAT acronym—Gratitude, Reflect, Exalt, Ask, and Trust—offers a flexible framework for morning prayer that engages your whole being:

1. **Gratitude** opens your heart to recognize God's gifts, shifting your focus from what's lacking to what's already been given.
2. **Reflection** creates space to examine your life in God's presence, allowing His light to illuminate both your growth and your need for grace.

3. **Exaltation** lifts your eyes from immediate concerns to eternal reality, declaring God's worthiness before facing the day's demands.
4. **Asking** acknowledges your dependence, bringing your needs to the One who delights to give good gifts to His children.
5. **Trusting** releases your grip on outcomes, surrendering the day ahead to the One whose wisdom and love exceed your own.

Together, these practices create a morning revolution—not just a change in schedule but a transformation in how you approach each new day. By beginning with God rather than immediately diving into tasks and concerns, you establish a foundation of grace that can sustain you through whatever challenges arise.

As you move forward from this study, remember that developing a consistent morning practice takes time. Be patient with yourself. Start small if necessary—even five minutes of focused attention on God is better than none. The goal isn't rigid adherence to a formula but growing relationship with the One who made you and loves you beyond measure.

Consider these practical steps for continuing your morning revolution:

1. **Establish a designated time and place** for morning prayer, creating environmental cues that support your practice.
2. **Begin the night before** by preparing for morning success—setting out materials, going to bed at a reasonable hour, and mentally committing to rising for this sacred appointment.
3. **Remove obstacles** that might prevent morning prayer, especially digital distractions that can hijack your attention.
4. **Find accountability** with a friend who shares your commitment to morning prayer, checking in regularly to encourage one another.
5. **Keep a journal** to record insights, prayers, and evidence of God's faithfulness, creating a written testimony of your journey.
6. **Extend grace to yourself** when you miss a morning, remembering that this is about relationship, not religious performance.

7. **Celebrate growth,** however small, recognizing that transformation happens through consistent, modest steps rather than dramatic leaps.

Above all, remember that the purpose of morning prayer is not to check off a spiritual box but to encounter the living God. Each morning offers a fresh opportunity to experience His mercies, which are "new every morning" (Lam. 3:23). As you cultivate the habit of beginning your day with God, may you discover the truth of the psalmist's words: "It is good to praise the LORD . . . proclaiming your love in the morning" (Ps. 92:1–2).

The morning revolution awaits—not a revolution of alarm clocks and willpower but a revolution of grace, presence, and transforming love. May God bless your journey as you rise to meet Him day by day.

"THE LORD'S PRAYER"

MATTHEW 6:9–13

This, then, is how you should pray:
"Our Father in heaven,
hallowed be your name,
10 your kingdom come,
your will be done,
on earth as it is in heaven.
11 Give us today our daily bread.
12 And forgive us our debts,
as we also have forgiven our debtors.
13 And lead us not into temptation,
but deliver us from the evil one."

LEADER'S GUIDE

If you are reading this, you have likely agreed to lead a group through *The GREAT Morning Revolution Bible Study*. Thank you! What you have chosen to do is important, and much good fruit can come from studies like this. The rewards of being a leader are different from those of participating, and we hope you find your own walk with Jesus deepened by this experience.

The GREAT Morning Revolution is a six-session prayer-practice Bible study built around video teaching content and small-group interaction. As the group leader, imagine yourself as the host of a dinner party . . . without dinner, unless, of course, that's your thing. Your job is to take care of your "guests" so that as they arrive, they feel comfortable and welcomed and excited to learn straightaway.

As the group leader, you are more of a facilitator than a teacher. Your role is NOT to answer all the questions or reteach the content. I, Tara Beth, am the teacher on video, and the study guide will prompt how the group experience will flow. Your job is to guide the experience and cultivate your small group into a learning and growing community. This will make it a place for members to process, question, reflect, and grow *together*.

There are several elements in this leader's guide that will help you as you structure your study and reflection time, so follow along and take advantage of each one.

BEFORE YOU BEGIN

Materials

Before your first meeting, make sure the participants have a copy of this study guide. Alternatively, you can hand out the study guides at your first meeting and give the group members some time to look over the material and ask any preliminary questions. During your first meeting, be sure to send a sheet around the room and have each member write down their name, phone number, and email address so you can keep in touch with them during the week.

Free Streaming Video Access

Additionally, spend a few minutes going over how to access the FREE streaming video using the code printed on the inside front cover of each study guide. Helping everyone understand how accessible this material is will go a long way if anyone (including you) has to miss a meeting or if any member of your group chooses to lead a study after the conclusion of this one!

A few commonly asked questions and answers:

Do I have to subscribe to StudyGateway? NO. If you sign up for StudyGateway for the first time using **studygateway.com/redeem,** you will *not* be prompted to subscribe, then or after.

Do I set up another account if I do another study later? NO. The next time you do a HarperChristian Resources study with FREE streaming access, all you need to do is enter the new access code, and the videos will be added to your account library.

There is a short video available walking you through how to access your streaming videos. You can choose to show the video at your first meeting or simply direct your group to the HarperChristian Resources YouTube channel to watch it at their convenience.

How to Access Free Steaming Videos: https://youtu.be/JPhG06ksOn8

Group Size

Generally, the ideal size for a group is between eight to ten people, which ensures everyone will have enough time to participate in discussions. If you have more people, you might want to break up the main group into smaller subgroups. Encourage those who show up at the first meeting to commit to attending for the duration of the study, as this will help the group members get to know each other, create stability for the group, and help you know how to prepare each week.

Opening

Each of the sessions begins with an opening icebreaker, a theological reflection, opening prayer, and a portion of Scripture that will be the focus of the teaching to read as a group.

Whenever prompted to select a volunteer to read a passage of any sort, please take the temperature of the room, as it were. Note the members of your group who do not readily raise their hand to volunteer. Reading Scripture aloud can incite anxiety or nervousness in some people. Please take the time in Week One to communicate the value of reading Scripture aloud as a community, in community. Encourage all your group members to try it at some point. Be clear that there is no bad reading of God's Word, rather it is *meant* to be read and shared with others. So, consider your group space a safe place to try and grow in this practice. One goal of this study is to grow participants in their overall engagement of God's Word, which includes feeling comfortable and confident with the words on the pages!

Preparing Your Group for the Study

Before watching your first video at your first meeting, let the group members know that each session in this study guide contains four days' worth of Bible study and a specific prayer practice on day five to complete during the week between group meetings. While we never want to make anyone feel obligated to engage with the personal study, it is written intentionally to help each person grow more comfortable with these aspects of daily morning prayer and will help your group members try all the practices presented to continue to shape their GREAT Morning Revolution experience. One of the most common aspects of all Christian life that people struggle with is prayer. It is my prayer and hope that you and your group will find new life in and desire for prayer to begin your every day through this study.

As always, invite your group members to bring any questions or insights they uncovered while studying or practicing each aspect of prayer to your next meeting, especially if they had a breakthrough moment or answered prayer or restored communication with God.

WEEKLY PREPARATION

As the leader, there are a few things you should do to prepare for each meeting:

- *Watch the video.* **This will help you to become familiar with the content you are presenting and give you foresight of what may or may not be brought up in the discussion time.**

- *Read through the group discussion section.* **This will help you to become familiar with the questions you will be asking, the focus Scripture, and the context. These** question prompts are written in an intentional order for the greatest learning and growth potential. If possible, plan to work through all the prompts as a group. Plan for the prompts you definitely want to cover if you run short on time.

- *Be prepared for potential responses or lack of engagement.* Every group has times when there are no respondents and the question falls flat out of the gate. This is normal and okay! Be prepared with YOUR answer to the questions so you can always offer to share as an icebreaker and example. **What you want to avoid is always answering the questions and therefore speaking for the group.** Foremost, encourage members of the group to answer questions.

- *Remind your group there are no wrong answers or dumb questions.* Note that in many cases there will not be one "right" answer to the question. Answers will vary, especially when the group members are being asked to share their personal experiences.

- *Pray for your group.* Pray for your group members throughout the week and ask God to lead them as they study His Word.

- *Bring extra supplies to your meeting.* The members should bring their own pens for writing notes, but it's a good idea to have extras available for those who forget. You may also want to bring paper and additional Bibles. If you find group members who are without a personal copy of the Bible, please invite them to let you know. There are a lot of great resources for low-cost outreach Bibles. You do not want anyone to be without a copy of the Bible if you can help it!

STRUCTURING THE DISCUSSION TIME

You will need to determine with your group how long you want to meet each week so you can plan your time accordingly. Generally, most groups like to meet for either sixty minutes or ninety minutes, so you could use one of the following schedules:

Section	60 minutes	90 minutes
• Introduction (members arrive and get settled; leader reads or summarizes introduction)	2 minutes	2 minutes
• Opening Activity	10 minutes	10 minutes
• Video Notes (watch the teaching video together and take notes)	20 minutes	20 minutes
• Group Discussion (discuss the Bible study questions)	25 minutes	55 minutes
• Closing Prayer (pray together as a group and dismiss)	3 minutes	3 minutes

As the group leader, it is up to you to keep track of the time and keep things moving along according to your schedule. You might want to set a timer for each segment so both you and the group members know when your time is up. (Note that there are some good phone apps for timers that play a gentle chime or other pleasant sound instead of a disruptive noise.)

Don't be concerned if the group members are quiet or slow to share. People are often quiet when they are pulling together their ideas, and this might be a new experience for them. Just ask a question and let it hang in the air until someone shares. You can then say, "Thank you. What about others? What came to you when you watched that portion of the video?"

GROUP DYNAMICS

Leading a group through *The GREAT Morning Revolution* will prove to be highly rewarding both to you and your group members. However, this doesn't mean you will not encounter any challenges along the way! Discussions can get off track. Group members may not be sensitive to the needs and ideas of others. Some might worry they will be expected to talk about matters that make them feel awkward. Others may express comments that result in disagreements. To help ease this strain on you and the group, consider the following ground rules:

- When someone raises a question or comment that is off the main topic, suggest you deal with it another time, or, if you feel led to go in that direction, let the group know you will be spending some time discussing it.
- If someone asks a question you don't know how to answer, admit it and move on. At your discretion, feel free to invite group members to comment on questions that call for personal experience.
- If you find one or two people are dominating the discussion time, direct a few questions to others in the group. Outside the main group time, ask the more dominating members to help you draw out the quieter ones. Work to make them a part of the solution instead of the problem.
- When a disagreement occurs, encourage the group members to process the matter *in love*. Encourage those on opposite sides to restate what they heard the other side say about the matter, and then invite each side to evaluate if that perception is accurate. Lead the group in examining other Scriptures related to the topic and look for common ground.

When any of these issues arise, encourage your group members to follow these words from the Bible: "Love one another" (John 13:34), "If it is possible, as far as it depends on you, live at peace with everyone" (Rom. 12:18), and "Be quick to listen, slow to speak and slow to become angry" (James 1:19). This will make your group time more rewarding and beneficial for everyone who attends.

SESSION-BY-SESSION OVERVIEWS

WEEK 1

JOY COMES IN THE MORNING

Scripture covered in this session: **Lamentations 3:19–26**

Inductive Study Scripture this week: **Lamentations 3:19–26; Psalm 5:1–8; Mark 1:29–39; Psalm 143:1–12**

Discussion Question choices / notes:

Prayer requests:

WEEK TWO

GRATITUDE: THE FOUNDATION OF MORNING PRAYER

Scripture covered in this session: **Psalm 92:1–2; 1 Thessalonians 5:16–18**

Inductive Study Scripture this week: **1 Thessalonians 5:16–18; Psalm 92:1–15; Philippians 4:4–9; Romans 1:18–25**

Discussion Question choices / notes:

Prayer requests:

WEEK THREE

REFLECT: LOOKING WITHIN AND LOOKING BACK

Scripture covered in this session: **Psalm 139:23–24; Lamentations 3:40**

Inductive Study Scripture this week: **Psalm 139:1–24; Psalm 77:1–20; Lamentations 3:37–42; James 1:19–25**

Discussion Question choices / notes:

Prayer requests:

WEEK FOUR

EXALT: LIFTING GOD'S NAME HIGH

Scripture covered in this session: **Psalm 34:1–3; Isaiah 6:1–5**

Inductive Study Scripture this week: **Psalm 34:1–10; 2 Corinthians 3:7–18; Habakkuk 3:17–19; Isaiah 6:1–8**

Discussion Question choices / notes:

Prayer requests:

WEEK FIVE

ASK: BRINGING OUR NEEDS TO GOD

Scripture covered in this session: **Matthew 7:7–11; Philippians 4:6–7**

Inductive Study Scripture this week: **Matthew 7:7–11; James 4:1–3; 1 Peter 5:5–11; Mark 11:20–25**

Discussion Question choices / notes:

Prayer requests:

WEEK SIX

TRUST: SURRENDERING OUR DAY TO GOD

Scripture covered in this session: **Proverbs 3:5–6; Isaiah 26:3–4**

Inductive Study Scripture this week: **Proverbs 3:5–7; Isaiah 26:1–4; Habakkuk 3:16–19; Matthew 6:25–34**

Discussion Question choices / notes:

Prayer requests:

ABOUT THE AUTHOR

Tara Beth Leach is a pastor, preacher of the Word, and writer. She speaks widely at conferences, retreats, and universities across the country on women in ministry, church leadership, and the call to be a radiant witness. She is the Senior Pastor at Good Shepherd Church in Naperville, Illinois, and previously served at Christ Church in Oak Brook and as Senior Pastor of First Church of the Nazarene of Pasadena ("PazNaz") in SoCal. She is a graduate of Olivet Nazarene University and Northern Theological Seminary and has authored three books, including *Emboldened* and *Radiant Church*. Tara Beth is the co-founder of Propel Ecclesia and is also the co-host of *The Pastors Table* podcast. She has two beautiful and rambunctious sons and has been married to the love of her life, Jeff, since 2006.

ALSO AVAILABLE

ZONDERVAN REFLECTIVE

BIBLE STUDY ON COVENANTS ALSO BY TARA BETH

From the Publisher

GREAT STUDIES

ARE EVEN BETTER WHEN THEY'RE SHARED!

Help others find this study:

- Post a review at your favorite online bookseller.
- Post a picture on a social media account and share why you enjoyed it.
- Send a note to a friend who would also love it—or, better yet, go through it with them.

Thanks for helping others grow their faith!